Tough Issues, Good Decisions

Lillian R. Putnam and Eileen M. Burke

SCHOLASTIC
PROFESSIONAL BOOKS

New York • Toronto • London • Auckland • Sydney
Mexico City • New Delhi • Hong Kong

To all the children who struggle
with ethical problems

Interior design by Drew Hires
Cover illustration by Jean-Claude Gotting
Interior illustrations by Gil Eisner
Cover design by Sue Kass
ISBN 0-439-24117-0

Acknowledgments

We are grateful to the following teachers who used some of the stories in *Tough Issues, Good Decisions* in their classrooms and were good enough to share the responses of their students with us:

Bonnie Cytron, fourth-grade teacher and Thelma Lydle and Dorothy Halloran, fifth-grade teachers in the Wildwood School in Mountain Lakes, New Jersey; Kathie Bush, fourth-grade teacher, Orchard Elementary School, Skillman, New Jersey; Marilyn Stebbins, sixth-grade teacher; Peter Colon, fourth-grade teacher and Alice Wellmon, fourth-grade teacher in the Challenger School, McGuire Air Force Base, McGuire, New Jersey; Elaine McGettigan, third-grade teacher in the Atlantis School, McGuire Air Force Base, McGuire, New Jersey. We offer a special thanks to Jacqueline Smith for her help in disseminating the stories for student response to the faculties of the Challenger and the Atlantis Schools. To all of those teachers who encouraged us to proceed and to their students who responded so honestly and thoughtfully to our stories, we are most appreciative.

—Lillian R. Putnam and Eileen M. Burke

Table of Contents

Introduction

Newspapers and other media are full of reports on ethical issues—from national scandals relating to banking and politics and school shootings, to local news articles announcing widespread cheating on standardized tests and drug use in schools and colleges.

Educators have realized that, for some time, the incidence and severity of violent crime in our schools have been increasing. This highlights a critical need to teach morals and ethics in school curricula. We refer not to specific religious beliefs but to ethical character, to "what you do when no one is looking," which is the way Robert Coles, the Harvard psychiatrist, has defined character.

Situations abound in classrooms that require decisions about what is right and what is best for the individual student and for all students. Students must deal with these situations. They do—oftentimes without reflection.

Problems involving values are often difficult to resolve. At times, they may require choosing between two equally desirable options. At other times, they may force a decision between equally undesirable choices. Losing a friend, being excluded from a group, losing self-respect for lack of courage or conviction are prices that may have to be paid when an ethical choice is made.

There are many reasons for taking class time to think through and talk about such problem situations.

First, children need a moral purpose in life as much as they need food, clothing, and shelter. Given this need, there is justification for helping children to develop an ethical consciousness.

Second, just as other basic needs are provided for at home and in school, it is here that moral purpose must be nurtured, guided, and shaped.

Third, emphasis on internal rather than external rewards is often acclaimed but less often practiced. Moral values depend upon internal rewards. Children who have observed the modeling and received the guidance that nurtures sound moral choices are less likely to be directed solely by tangible rewards.

Fourth, ethical choices confront all people throughout their lives: whether or not to report dishonesty; whether to claim the work of another as one's own; whether lying is an option in the name of preserving friendship. Children as well as adults face these and many other questions. The need for decisions in such situations is lifelong.

Fifth, reading about and discussing class and school situations in which ethical decisions are needed, lead to the identification of problems, factors contributing to them, alternate responses to them, solutions, and fresh insights. Critical thinking is sharpened, values are shaped, and ethical awareness is strengthened.

Sixth, a class which together probes situations that call for a sensitivity to what is for the good of all and the good of each member, is a class whose awareness level has been raised. Students in such a class will not gloss over future situations dealing with moral issues and behaviors as they occur in the classroom and in the school. The respect for each other that develops through such group engagement with ethical issues has lifelong benefits and an extensive outreach. Developing respect for one another is also a step toward making crimes against justice far less likely.

Seventh, it is in dealing with questions of values and ethics that character is fashioned. Without thought and discussion given to the ethical dilemmas that we face each day, decisions regarding them are not likely to become easier, clearer, or fairer. Honesty, courage, self-discipline, dependability, sensitivity, respect, kindness, a sense of justice, and like behaviors are more likely to develop when situations involving them are allotted discussion time in the home and in the school. Character formation depends upon wrestling with such situations and dealing with the choices available. A sense of right and wrong is sharpened as students grapple with such problems.

Eighth, stories such as these provide teachers with situations enough like actual school experiences to be highly relevant to everyday school life. At the same time, vicarious as they are, they provide the distancing that may be needed to discuss them fully and openly. It has been our experience that stories are an excellent vehicle for confronting and discussing problems.

Ninth, reflection on such situations helps us to know ourselves better. Engaging in talk about a character in a classroom and school situation who is faced with an ethical dilemma, and thus, with an ethical decision, is to place the student in the character's predicament. When this happens, both the mind and the emotions of the student are captured. The impact is likely to be strong, and self-knowledge is deepened.

Teacher's Guide

The stories in *Tough Issues, Good Decisions* reflect classroom and school life. They represent situations you and your students can and do encounter as you go about living and working with each other.

The stories deal with such behaviors as lying, cheating, plagiarizing, stealing, using drugs, pulling pranks, bullying, making hasty judgments, vandalism, being intolerant, name-calling, and being prejudiced.

The story method has long been an effective means by which to involve children in reflecting upon a learning situation or problem. Such reflection is strengthened by identification with characters who grapple with situations that are well-known to students.

Throughout the discussion of these stories, you will want to create a climate in which students realize that the values of all people are formed by their parents, homes, origins, and personal experiences.

STORY PRESENTATION

It is preferable to allow students to read the story first individually, then reflect upon it, and finally discuss it. Discussion with peers is likely to trigger multiple ideas and solutions, and to reveal fresh insights. Specifically, you may find the following sequence useful. Students:

1. read or listen to a story with an ethical problem.
2. reflect on the story. You may wish to give them a few minutes to think silently about the story.
3. identify the problem(s).
4. propose alternate solutions.
5. evaluate the consequences of each solution individually and in groups.
6. justify the choices they make.
7. extend the discussion through language arts activities such as the following:
   • writing personal stories
   • writing responses to the story before discussion
   • debating consequences of alternate solutions
   • placing the characters in cartoon frames to explain the problem
   • creating spin-offs for similar stories
   • exploring drama possibilities by placing the story in a courtroom setting.

You will want to provide time for students to discuss similar situations in their own lives. It is in connecting stories, such as those in this book, with their own experiences that students will feel most strongly the impact of these problem situations. You know the connection with their own lives is being made when students comment, "That happened to me once," or "My brother got in the same kind of trouble," or "We had a kid like that in our class last year."

GUIDES FOR DISCUSSION

You will want to be certain that:

1. each student is given a chance to express an opinion regardless of the nature of the opinion.
2. one student talks at a time.
3. all students listen respectfully, even if they disagree.

The questions in the book need not necessarily be taken in order. Sometimes two or three questions will be under discussion simultaneously, as they impinge on each other. This is perfectly acceptable, and it is wise to allow the discussion to proceed in a natural fashion. For the most part, questions are open-ended to allow for considerable thought and talk. If, however, the discussion does not "move along" well enough to sustain interest, you can probe or insert leading questions or suggestions.

There are many ways to use the questions. You may choose to:

• *use them sequentially as printed.*

At times, questions focus on different characters; at other times, the experiences are of one character; and at still other times, on facets of the situation. Using

them sequentially may help to explore the situation in depth.

• *use them selectively as seems appropriate in terms of class interest or need.*

Class or school events or the sharing of a recent book may lead to a particularly timely question. You may choose to hone in on this one.

• *use them selectively based on students' targeted purposes and interests.*

As the story is completed and the discussion begins, it may become clear that your students are interested in a specific character, specific behavior, or special aspect of the situation. It is wise to recognize such interest and attention.

• *add to the questions in order to accommodate additional ideas.*

You will find as discussion proceeds and experiences of students are linked to story events that new questions, comments, and views will be identified, and additional questions will be needed to ferret out a full range of responses to the story.

• *organize the questions singly or in clusters and assign them to individuals or groups of students.*

Questions may sometimes be handled best by small groups or individual students who concentrate on one or two aspects of the situation. Time for group sharing with the entire class would follow.

• *use your own set of questions.*

The prompt questions included at the end of each story may stir your thinking and nurture a whole new set of questions. Do not hesitate to use those. You know best the pertinence of each story to your class and the questions that might best stir discussion and debate.

Also, be sure to ask your students to think of questions. You should serve as discussion leader to insure equal participation by all your students. It is possible, however, that after your students have had sufficient experience with the stories and discussions, you may wish to assign a student to the role of discussion leader.

Since you are asking students to discuss what they think about these ethical issues, you may receive a variety of responses. If groups of students arrive at "unethical" answers or conclusions and appear to be satisfied with those conclusions, you might direct their attention to consideration of the consequences for everyone—both short and long term. This tactic usually frees up a more ethical approach.

At times, it may be helpful to break in the middle of the discussion. Sometimes the interval of a night or day provides thinking time that results in a more thoughtful, rational approach.

We realize that consciousness-raising does not happen immediately. It takes time to develop. These stories will help students become more conscious of ethical issues, and the discussions following them will provide the motivation to continue giving thought and reflection to these lifelong problems.

After discussing these stories, some students may wish to write stories of their own, perhaps from personal experience. If students agree, the sharing of such personal stories would be particularly pertinent and rich in furthering the development of ethical consciousness. An integration of all the language arts is achieved when students listen to, read, discuss, and respond in writing to the stories. In order to do this we have included a writing prompt following each set of questions at the end of each story.

ORDER OF STORIES

Although the problems involved in all these stories are faced by children of all ages, the following stories seem to be more appropriate, but do not need to be limited to grades 4, 5, and 6:

Class Klutz
The Clarion News
Which Clown?
"You Owe Me."
Cupcakes, Paper, and Paste
The Cafeteria
Incident at the Water Fountain
"I'm Sick of Hearing Her...."
The Babysitter
Stopwatch
The Fire Drill

The following stories seem to be more useful, but do not need to be limited to grades 6, 7, and 8:

Slam Dunk
Flying Eagle
Lost Programs?
Art Gone Awry
No Limit on Wit
Raising the Hoop
The White Stuff
The Contract
Silent Witness
How Do You Say, "No"?
The Softball Team

BOOKS FOR DISCUSSION

Plots that center on ethical problems are bountiful in children's literature. In the section Suggestions for Further Reading and Discussion, 19 books are cited along with a brief annotation and guide questions. In all cases, the books provide a depth and breadth of tale that the brevity of the stories does not allow. There are, therefore, many more discussion topics and potential questions for each book than are provided here. Each book will invite several days of rich discussion.

EVALUATION

How can the results of a project of this nature be evaluated? Certainly no standardized test can do it. Rather you would look for a change in classroom behavior that progresses from an awareness of ethical issues, to the identification of problems, to the analysis of consequences of decisions, and on to responsible action.

Children are most clearly acting responsibly when they stand up for an ethical principle. Ethical actions may be observed in the classroom by an increase in:

- reflection on the consequences of one's behavior.
- sensitivity and respect for the property and feelings of others.
- a willingness to deliberate rather than to fight.
- tolerance for differing opinions.
- an appreciation of internal rather than external rewards.

If the study of these stories has been effective, there should be an increase in moral conduct, which will affect everything students do and say—even, as Robert Coles asserts, "when no one is looking."

Class Klutz

Susan and Charlie have been taking care of the class earth science exhibits during Science Fair days. The models and explanations of volcanoes, earthquakes, and the effects of glaciation stand tall in boxes and on bases of many sizes and forms.

Today, after making certain that the exhibits and their labels are visible and in order, Susan and Charlie return to playing word games at their Word Learning Center. Neither of them sees their classmate, Scott, take a sudden turn and bump against one of the exhibit tables. Several exhibits are upset. Looking up from their word games, Susan and Charlie see what's happened.

Scott looks very embarrassed; he tries to right the models and restore the labels while Susan and Charlie shake their heads and both remark, "That's Scott for you!" Scott blushes even more when Charlie pushes him and says, "You're so clumsy, Scott. Get away."

Then Susan complains, "And we just finished straightening up the exhibits for the fifth graders' visit."

Sarah, looking at the messed-up table, sings out, "Scott is so-o-o-o clumsy."

Then George pipes in. "I guess every class has to have a klutz. Yesterday, he ruined our mural by stepping on it."

"Class Klutz. That's a good name for him," says Judy, who thought her best art work had been ruined by Scott's misstep on the mural.

Scott hears all of these remarks and thinks that if only they had painted their mural in the back of the room out of the way, nobody would have stepped on it. Unhappy, he walks to the class Book Nook to be by himself.

It takes him a while to select a book. In the meantime, he has upset several shelves. Nancy joins him in the Book Nook looking for a special poem. She notices the disorder of the shelves and complains, "Oh, Scott, can't you do anything right? Look at the mess you've made. Now I'll never find what I want."

Angrily, Scott replies, "Well, I was just going to start to put the books back."

Even more angrily, Nancy retorts, "When, next year?"

With his book in his hand, Scott, angry and thoroughly depressed, walks as far away from everyone as he can. He wonders unhappily if he's really going to be known as the "Class Klutz"? Slouching in his chair, Scott looks sad and defeated.

QUESTIONS FOR DISCUSSION

1. Have you or your friends ever invented a name for someone who seems to cause problems in the classroom?

2. Did this name-calling help solve the problems?

3. Did the name-calling help the person given the name?

4. If Scott becomes known as "Class Klutz," how do you think he will behave in the future?

5. What do you think Scott should do in this situation?

6. What do you think about the behavior of Scott's classmates?

7. Would you like to help Scott be less klutzy? What specifically could you do to help him?

WRITE ABOUT IT

Pretend that when you were in the third grade, some of your classmates called you "a wimp." You were very unhappy about this, so you understand how Scott might be feeling. Describe your feelings and your actions at that time.

The Clarion News

The fifth graders' newspaper, *The Clarion News*, came out every other month. The January/February issue was being assembled.

There was always a joke column that everyone enjoyed. Bill had submitted several ideas for the joke column to the editor, Zoe, but was told that everyone already knew these jokes.

Bill really wanted his name to appear in the paper and tried to write a joke on his own. Finally, he submitted a "Where do you find…" joke.

Question: *Where do you find elephants?*

Answer: *It all depends on where you put them.*

Zoe grinned when Bill shared the joke with her, but she said, "You need more than that for the column."

Bill sighed and thought about the funny joke the teacher shared last week:

Question: *What do you have when an owl and a goat get together?*

Answer: *A Hootenanny.*

The teacher, Ms. Wells, had said that lots of jokes come from playing with words. Bill thought he could play with words too. He rotated his pencil in his hand again and again as he thought. Nothing seemed to come to him quickly, and this was the very last day students could submit anything to the editor.

As Bill sat frowning over his pencil,

his eyes roamed around the room and rested on one of the library shelves where copies of old newspapers from last year's class were stacked. Ms. Wells kept these for students to use. Bill knew that there were jokes in each issue, and he walked over to the shelf and leafed through a few issues.

He found himself laughing at several of the jokes and thinking they were really funny. He was also thinking that the class wouldn't know these jokes.

Suddenly Bill found himself wondering why he couldn't copy one and submit it to the editor. He found one that he especially liked, copied it, signed it, and handed it to Zoe with the "Where-do-you-find-elephants?" joke.

Zoe said, "Great!" The January/February issue of *The Clarion News* carried Bill's name under both jokes.

QUESTIONS FOR DISCUSSION

1. What do you think of Bill's behavior?

2. What other actions might Bill have taken to appear in *The Clarion News*?

3. If you found something you wished to share with others—jokes or poems or special paragraphs—how might you do this?

4. The person who wrote the joke in the newspaper will not know that Bill claimed the joke as his. Is there any harm then in what Bill did?

5. If the joke Bill found was unsigned, is there any reason he cannot claim it as his own?

WRITE ABOUT IT

You are the author of the joke Bill found in the copy of the old newspaper. You discover that Bill has claimed your joke as his own. Write about how this would make you feel and why.

Which Clown?

In Center School, Halloween was a day of surprises, fun, and mystery. Everyone wore costumes and sometimes masks. Guessing who the masqueraders were was the game of the day.

In Mr. Selski's class, there were several clowns. Tamara was one. Her mask sported a Pinocchio-sized nose and a big, red mouth. On her head, she wore a bright orange wig. Tamara was not the only clown, but she couldn't guess which of her friends were wearing clown costumes.

At Center School, it was the custom for the older classes to pair with a class of younger children to view one another's costumes and to share refreshments. Tamara was enjoying herself. She stood laughing at one of the little children who was wearing a monster costume and was trying to look ferocious while eating a cookie.

Suddenly, she heard a cry behind her and turned to see a little "dinosaur" topple over. She ran to help the child up when she heard the young children who were standing near the fallen dinosaur yell, "She's a bad clown, a bad clown!" while pointing to a tall child in a clown's costume leaving the room.

The teacher of the young children, Mrs. Simcox, walked over to Tamara and the small dinosaur who, by this time, was crying loudly. Hearing the chant, "Bad clown, bad clown!" Mrs. Simcox looked at Tamara and asked, "What happened?" At the same time, she helped the little dinosaur up, saying, "That's all right, David, everything will be all right."

Again, Mrs. Simcox turned to Tamara and waited for an answer.

Tamara replied, "I don't know. I heard someone cry and turned around and saw him." She pointed to the small dinosaur.

David, by this time, was crying even more loudly while the other children kept chanting, "Bad clown, bad clown!" Seeing no other clowns, Mrs. Simcox, clearly annoyed, said, "Well, you must have done something!"

"The clown pushed him down," yelled one small voice. David, by this time, was totally incoherent. His dinosaur tail was ruined, and he couldn't control his tears enough to answer any of Mrs. Simcox's questions.

In frustration, Mrs. Simcox turned to Tamara and said, "You older children should have enough sense to take care of young children like David."

Tamara protested, "But—"

With an exasperated look at Tamara, Mrs. Simcox marched off holding David by the hand.

Mr. Selski, seeing only a very upset Mrs. Simcox escorting David out of the room, walked over to Tamara and asked, "What happened?"

Tamara, upset herself, answered that she really didn't know, but she thought Mrs. Simcox blamed her for whatever had happened.

QUESTIONS FOR DISCUSSION

1. Has anything like that ever happened to you?

2. Should Tamara make a point of talking to Mrs. Simcox later to try to explain the situation?

3. Should Tamara speak with the other small children and have them help her explain to Mrs. Simcox what really happened?

4. What do you think about Mrs. Simcox's behavior?

5. What can Tamara learn from this situation?

6. If you were Tamara, what would you do now?

WRITE ABOUT IT

You can probably remember a number of times when you have been blamed by your parents, brother, sister, teacher, or others for something you did not do. List any reasons you can think of that explain why the blame was placed on you. How did you react to these false accusations?

"You Owe Me."

Carlos walked along the sidewalk as slowly as he possibly could. He took time to kick every stone in sight. He kicked the stones for blocks—anything to delay his arrival at school. Today was Friday, and the teacher had announced that she would be giving the big history test this morning.

Carlos wasn't prepared. He hadn't studied at all. It wasn't that he didn't want to study and work, but there just wasn't time to do it. He was the best player on the soccer team, so he really had to play all the games. He also was the best hitter on the softball team, so he really had to be there for every game. If he didn't, he'd be letting the school down, and he couldn't do that. They were depending on him. No, he had to be there. But that left him no time to study, and today was the big test.

Maybe the teacher will be absent, Carlos thought. Then there would be no test. His hopes soared for a moment, but then he realized this teacher was never absent. If the electricity went off, she would teach by candlelight. If the heat went off, she would tell everybody to wear sweaters. There was no chance of her not being in class.

Then suddenly Carlos thought of Paul. Paul was smart. He always got good marks on tests. He always knew all the answers—even the hard ones. Paul would probably have spent a lot time studying, and would know the answers. Maybe

Paul would help him just this once.

Carlos walked along faster now. He would speak to Paul before school and ask him to help him, just this once. Paul sat directly opposite from Carlos, so it would be easy for Paul to push his paper to one side of his desk, and Carlos could look over to see the answers. He wouldn't copy all the right answers because that might look suspicious. He wanted just enough right answers to pass.

Carlos spotted Paul entering the school building. He pulled him aside and explained his problem. He told Paul about how much time he had been giving to school sports and, with no time to study, he could fail the test. Paul listened silently until Carlos had told the whole story, and then he looked Carlos straight in the eye and said firmly, "No way, no way!" Then he pushed past Carlos and went into the school building.

Carlos was angry and shaken. Not only wouldn't Paul help him when he needed it, but he didn't even care that

Carlos had been spending all his spare time helping the school in games. Now what would he do?

At that moment Ashley walked past and said, "Hi, Carlos. Are you going in?"

"Yeah," answered Carlos. As they walked along the corridor together, Carlos started to think. Ashley was a nice kid, full of fun, and always nice to be with. Maybe she would help. She wasn't a top student, just kind of average, but maybe she would pass the history test. Best of all, she sat directly in front of him in the history class. It was worth a try, he thought.

Carlos slowly told Ashley how hard he had worked on the school teams to help the school. He told her how many hours he had spent practicing, and that there was no time left to study. Of course she already knew about the history test today. Then he quietly asked her if she would "share" some of her answers with him. He explained that since she sat directly in front of him, if she just placed her paper on the side of her desk and moved her body to the other side, he could see her answers easily.

Ashley looked surprised at first, but as Carlos continued to talk about how easily it could be done, she looked serious and thoughtful.

"Well, it's not fair," she said. "You did so much for the school you had no time for yourself. Well, maybe, just this once, but only once."

They took the exam and, true to her word, Ashley slid her paper to the edge of the desk and moved herself to the opposite side so Carlos could see the answers.

What they didn't know was that Paul saw all this and guessed what was going on. As Paul walked out of the classroom after finishing the exam, he felt angry and confused. What should he do? Should he tell Carlos that he knew he had taken Ashley's answers? Should he tell Ashley that he knew she had helped Carlos? Should he tell the teacher what he saw? What was the right thing to do?

QUESTIONS FOR DISCUSSION

1. Pretend that you are Paul. When Paul refused to help Carlos during the exam, he must have had some good reasons. What do you think his reasons were?

2. If someone asked Ashley why she agreed to help Carlos, what reasons do you think she would have given? Do you agree with her?

3. Do you think Carlos had a right to ask for help because he spent so much time playing for the school? If you don't agree, how could you explain this to Carlos?

4. Have you ever been in a situation similar to that of Paul or Ashley? What did you decide to do? Why?

WRITE ABOUT IT

List ways you think a school might help students who are good in sports to stay on top of their studies. Then list ways you think students can keep up with their school work while being active in sports programs.

Cupcakes, Paper, and Paste

"If you can get away with it, why not? Who's going to know? Nobody's going to miss a few boxes of cupcakes," Ron asserted. "It's like my mom and dad do with their income tax. If you can get away with it, why mention it? My dad gets a lot of fees 'under the table' he calls it. Nobody knows the difference."

Jasmine stared. "But it's wrong. It's not honest," she said.

"It's not hurting anybody. Why worry?" Ron asked.

"But somebody has to pay for those cupcakes. They don't come free," argued Jasmine.

"The school system pays for them. It's not out of our pocket. Come on! I'm hungry and nobody's watching."

Ron walked to the cafeteria stock-room where he knew the boxes of cupcakes were kept and stuffed several packages into his backpack. Jasmine didn't follow him but instead started for her next class. Ron was right; nobody was watching. Nobody knew about the lost cupcakes but her.

Jasmine thought a lot about Ron and his "nobody's watching" comment. She began to notice a number of things she and her classmates did when nobody was watching.

Projects were popular in her school, and lots of materials were needed to complete them. When she was supply monitor, she noticed how much paint, paper, paste, and other art supplies were taken home. It seemed to be much more than anyone would really need. When her friend Shannon needed some tagboard, there was none on the shelf. The teacher seemed puzzled because so much had been ordered. Jasmine thought she knew why none was left.

She noticed too that the paperbacks that teachers ordered so each student could have one as they shared a story sometimes decreased in number over a month or so. She had heard more than one classmate say, "Oh well, I guess I lost it, but they have plenty of copies." Embarrassed, she thought about the time she had said the same thing.

Jasmine wondered if Ron were right. Nobody watched; nobody cared. The supply was always there. But no. That wasn't so. Shannon didn't find the tagboard when she needed it, and the next class that shared *Shiloh* would be short a copy or two.

Why should she care? Jasmine shrugged and tried to dismiss the concern although she talked about it with Shannon.

May 1 arrived, and it was time for the annual Art Show and Young Authors' Conference. Everybody enjoyed these. Ms. Marks was a great art teacher, and their school was known for its exceptional show. All the teachers and students contributed to the Young Authors' Conference, and bound books were displayed everywhere.

Personally, Jasmine was looking forward to seeing her charcoal drawing exhibited. Ms. Marks had helped her with it, and Jasmine was so proud of it. She couldn't wait to see it framed and hung.

The school took pride in both the Art Show and Young Authors' programs and always gave the exhibit a very professional look.

Shannon and Jasmine were surprised, therefore, when they entered the all-purpose room to find no framed artwork. All the work was attached with paperclips to string extending from one wall of the room to the opposite side. Somehow it was very disappointing.

Jasmine heard parents ask Ms. Marks about the frames and also heard comments about the books that weren't bound in the same materials as in previous years. Replies from teachers were the same—the supply budget had been exhausted early because of all the projects the students were continuously engaged in. Parents looked puzzled. So did the students who expected their work to be exhibited in the usual finished fashion.

The principal and teachers received so many comments from parents and visitors and the students themselves about the show and the conference not being "quite what it used to be" that they began to think about the vanishing supplies. One or two also remarked about the dwindling paperbacks.

"Well," said one teacher, "you can't have children working on as many activities as we have in our school and not expect that materials will be used up. And you can't have children reading so many different books and not have some missing. It looks like we really have to budget more money for materials and paperbacks next year."

The principal looked worried at this comment. She knew her school already spent more money on supplies than any other school in the district.

Shannon's mother was an officer in the parent association in the school. Shannon heard her mother mention the need for more money next year and comment that she "didn't know where it would come from." Shannon called Jasmine, and they tried to decide if they should talk to the principal about some of the things that Jasmine had noticed.

QUESTIONS FOR DISCUSSION

1. What do you think about Ron's comments? If nobody is watching, is there anything wrong in taking a few cupcakes that "nobody will ever miss?"

2. Jasmine did see Ron take cupcakes, but she only thought she knew why paper, paint, tagboard, and other supplies were missing. Since she didn't know for a fact that students had taken them needlessly, should Jasmine share this information with Shannon's mother?

3. Why should Jasmine feel any concern or responsibility about the missing supplies?

4. If you were Jasmine, would you advise Shannon to tell her mother about the observations she (Jasmine) has made? If not, what would you do?

5. Jasmine saw Ron take the cupcakes. She also knew that he expected her to follow him. She was troubled by the fact that he thought she would join him. Should she report Ron? Should she try to find out why he thought she would follow him into the supply room and steal cupcakes too?

WRITE ABOUT IT

After reading "Cupcakes, Paper, and Paste," notice, over a period of several days, the quantity of school supplies you and your classmates use. Is it all necessary? Write arguments you might use to persuade your classmates to judge better the amount of materials they need. Consider the effect that better estimating might make in classroom programs and activities.

The Cafeteria

Natisha was humming as she skipped down the hall. She was very happy. Today was Thursday, and she and her best friend Katie had the same lunch period. That meant they could sit together and talk for almost an hour.

Katie and she had so many things in common. They were on the same soccer team, so they attended all the games and practices together. They also sang in the chorus, so they went to all the rehearsals together. There was just so much to talk about. Having a really good friend made Natisha very happy.

As Natisha entered the cafeteria, she saw that Katie was already in line, so Natisha picked up a tray and moved in behind her. "Hi," said Katie, and she motioned for Natisha to follow her. Katie selected a slice of pizza, a glass of milk, and a piece of chocolate cake. That looked good to Natisha, so she chose the same.

"Let's sit over by the windows," suggested Katie. Natisha nodded her head in agreement. When they got to the end of the line where the cashier was sitting, they suddenly heard something crash to the ground. It was a glass bowl and it had broken into a thousand pieces.

"Oh, someone could get hurt," said the cashier. "Let me pick this up." She bent over the floor with her head beneath the counter. She started to pick up the pieces of broken glass.

At that moment, Natisha saw to her amazement that Katie walked right past

the cashier's desk and over to the table area. Natisha didn't know exactly what was happening. Had Katie forgotten to pay for her lunch? Did she think she had already paid for it? Natisha stood there in a daze, not knowing exactly what to do. Should she call out to Katie and remind her to pay the cashier? Would that embarrass Katie? Or should she walk over and tell her?

When the cashier got up from the floor, she looked at Natisha's tray, and said, "Seventy-five cents, please." Natisha paid the cashier. Somehow the cashier didn't seem to realize that Katie had skipped out without paying.

As Natisha sat down and began to eat her pizza, she said to Katie, "Katie, you didn't pay for your lunch. Did you forget?"

"No," replied Katie. "She didn't ask me for it."

"But you knew she was cleaning up the glass underneath the counter. She couldn't see you after you left."

"It doesn't matter," replied Katie. "If

she had asked me, I would have paid for it, but she didn't so I didn't!" Katie spoke as if she had just made a courtroom decision.

Natisha toyed with her pizza. Somehow it didn't seem so appetizing now. Even the chocolate cake had no appeal. She sat silently for a few minutes. What had gone wrong? This was supposed to be such a nice, happy time—a time to talk about soccer, the chorus, and all the fun things they were doing together. Now she didn't feel like talking about anything.

Natisha glanced over at Katie. Katie was finishing her pizza and starting on her chocolate cake. She seemed completely unconcerned.

How could she have done this, wondered Natisha. Katie stole, and she knows it. Just because the cashier was looking down is no excuse. It's still stealing. She knows it. I know it. We both know it.

But Katie was her best friend. How could she be friends with someone who was dishonest? Natisha made one more try. She asked Katie to return to the cashier and tell her she forgot to pay her for the lunch. In that way, they could start all over again, and maybe Katie wouldn't do it again.

"No way," said Katie vehemently. "She didn't ask me, so I didn't pay. I didn't do anything wrong."

Natisha tried a few more ways to get Katie to go back and pay for the lunch because she really wanted them to stay good friends. Talking together and being together wouldn't be fun anymore. There would be a wall between them. Finally Natisha picked up her tray, murmured something about getting back to class, and left the cafeteria.

Natisha felt awful. The day was ruined. Was she being too hard on Katie? After all, Katie was right when she said that the cashier didn't actually ask her for the money. Natisha felt confused and upset. Should she ruin a perfectly good friendship because of this one lunch?

QUESTIONS FOR DISCUSSION

1. Was Katie dishonest in not paying for the lunch? Pretend you are Katie, and argue for her side.

2. Have you ever seen a friend do something like this? What did you do about it?

3. Is honesty a "given," something that doesn't change regardless of the circumstances? Or are there certain conditions that change it?

4. Someone once said, "If you can get away with anything, that makes it O.K." Do you agree with that?

WRITE ABOUT IT

Friendship is precious. Katie and Natisha really enjoy each other. Think about the times you and a good friend disagreed because you thought he or she did something "not quite right." What did you do? Was your reaction something that Natisha and Katie might learn from? As you think back, is there anything you might have done differently to solve the problem and keep the friendship?

Incident at the Water Fountain

Practice had been great that day. Although it was hot as blazes, the boys played as hard as they could. Their soccer skills were really improving. They all felt great—like real winners.

"Time for a drink," shouted the coach, and they all headed for the drinking fountain near the school building. Twelve boys raced from the field, each hoping to reach the fountain first. They all were hot and sweaty, and perspiration ran down the backs of their necks.

Ed could hardly wait for that nice, cool water to flow down his throat and to trickle over his hot face and neck. He ran as fast as he could and because he was such a fast runner, he arrived at the fountain first. He was just about to bend down over the drinking fountain when he heard a gruff, loud voice behind him saying, "Not so fast, shrimp, I'm first here."

Ed looked up to see Gil standing right behind him. Gil was the biggest boy in the class. He was as big as a kid in high school. He practiced weightlifting and was always showing everyone his muscles.

Ed stood his ground. "No, I'm first," he said. "I got here first so I get to drink first." Ed didn't move.

Gil moved a step closer, looking more threatening than ever. "You don't understand, shorty," replied Gil. "I'm always first whether I get there first or not. That's the way it is because I say so! Now get out of my way."

By this time all of the team and other

students were standing there, watching what was happening, but no one said a word. Why aren't they backing me up, wondered Ed. Why are they just standing there and watching? Why don't they say or do something?

Ed stood his ground. He told Gil that they all had a chance to race to the fountain and that since he got there first, he should have the first drink. But Gil was stubborn.

"This is the last time I'm going to tell you, shrimp," said Gil. "Move aside or you'll be sorry."

Ed pretended he didn't hear and leaned over the fountain to take that much-needed drink of water, but Gil reached over, grabbed Ed by the collar, and banged his head against the metal water faucet. The bang made everyone jump. Ed yelled with pain as his head hit the hard metal and his forehead started to bleed. He fell backwards on the ground, almost in a dead faint.

Gil stepped up to the fountain and calmly took a long drink. Then he said, "The rest of you kids just remember I'm always first in everything. Everything. And that's because I say so!"

Gil turned around, glanced down at Ed on the ground, and said, "He'll remember that next time." Then he smirked, let out a mean laugh, and went into the school building.

As Ed lay on the ground, things looked dark and foggy. Some of the other kids came up to see if he was all right. Two friends offered to walk home with him and gave him some paper towels to put on the cut. It was bleeding so much he knew he should go home and have his mother fix it. But he hated to do that. She would think he had been fighting, and he hadn't. He was right to drink first; he knew he was. Ed hadn't done anything to Gil. And what about the other kids? Why had they stood there and not done anything? They let him stand up to Gil all by himself. A fine pack of friends they were! If they had all ganged up on Gil, they could have stopped him. Separately, no one could fight back against Gil, but all together they could. All these thoughts crowded Ed's mind until he felt dizzy with so many unanswered questions.

When he arrived home, his mother was out, so he washed and cleaned the cut and put a small bandage over it. Then he pulled his hair down over his forehead so it didn't show too much. Fortunately, no one noticed it at home.

The next morning Ed went to school as usual. The very first thing in the morning, the teacher said there was something she wanted to discuss with the class. No one moved or said anything. Everyone knew what it would be about. Somebody had told her something. She asked first if anyone wanted to tell what happened after practice. No one raised a hand. She probed further and asked if anyone was hurt. Ed knew she was trying to get to the bottom of this. He knew that if the other kids told what had happened, Gil would find out and then they would get hurt too. If he told what had happened, Gil would be after him again.

Ed sat in his seat squirming. He didn't know what to do. Should he speak up and tell what happened? He certainly would like to see Gil get punished for what he did, but what would be the consequences?

QUESTIONS FOR DISCUSSION

1. Has anything like this ever happened to you? What did you do about it?
2. What kind of a person is Gil? What is a good word to describe him?
3. Do the other children at the water fountain bear any responsibility for what happened to Ed? If so, what?
4. If Gil is allowed to get away this time, what will happen the next time?
5. If you were a member of the group who had witnessed the incident, what would you do? Why?

WRITE ABOUT IT

You are a member of your school's Student Council. The Council has been concerned about some of the bullies in the building. You think about this and decide to list ways the Council and school might deal with "bullying."

"I'm Sick of Hearing Her."

"I know she always brags, but everyone else knows she does it too. Why let it bother you? Just forget it," Rosie said.

"I'm not going to forget it. I'm sick of it. Like her house, it's always so big and beautiful and better than anyone else's. Did you ever hear such garbage? You'd think she'd get tired of hearing herself brag about everything," Annie replied.

"Well, maybe she's telling the truth. I never thought her clothes were anything special, but I've never been to her house. Have you?" asked Kareem.

"I don't have to go to her house to know it doesn't have marble floors and four bathrooms and a special fitness room," retorted Annie. "She's a liar."

Jack passed by as Rosie, Kareem, and Annie talked and wondered who they were calling a liar. Then he heard Kareem say, "Well, maybe Abby is like some people who need to lie because real life is so hard for them. Don't you remember how many stories we've heard where someone creates imaginary adventures because life is so dull, or hard, or—"

Abby? Jack thought. He didn't know Abby well at all but if she were lying because life was so hard, he would really like to know more about it. He was on his way to meet Ramon; they were going to the playing field to practice pitching and catching.

Ramon and he practiced for a while, and then they sat down for a couple of

minutes. It was then Jack remembered what he had heard.

"Hey, did you know that Abby lies a lot because her life is so hard? I heard Annie call her a liar and say something about her life being so hard. Do you know Abby?

Ramon said, "Not really. But I never thought she was a liar. She must live in a great house though from what she says, so I don't buy the bit about life being hard."

"I wonder what she lies about. Is it her house?" asked Jack. "Whatever it is, Annie seemed fed up with her."

On the way home, the boys saw Abby walking on the other side of the street holding a small child in each hand. Both children were very young and well dressed.

"There she is," said Ramon. "I didn't

know she had any sisters or brothers." After walking a few blocks in the same direction, the boys saw Abby enter a large, expensive-looking house. "Well," said Ramon, "She certainly isn't lying about the great house she lives in. That's huge!"

The next day, Jack and Ramon were coming from the cafeteria as Abby entered it. Ramon said, "Your house is something else, Abby. You and your sisters and brothers certainly should have plenty of room to play in it."

Abby looked puzzled and said, "Sisters and brothers? I don't have any sisters and brothers, and my house is ... "

Others were forcing their way around them to enter the cafeteria so the three separated and moved away—Abby confused, and Jack and Ramon looking at each other and mouthing the word, "Liar."

"Who's a liar?" asked Nick, noting the exchange between Jack and Ramon. In no time the word got around the cafeteria that Abby was "a liar."

Abby began to feel the stares of everyone and wondered what was wrong.

Later, Ramon, still puzzled, insisted to Jack, "That house was huge. No brothers or sisters? Could they be the neighbor's kids? She treated them as though she knew them really well—as though they definitely belonged together."

Jack shook his head and said, "Why would she lie?" Ramon shrugged his shoulders.

That afternoon, Abby returned the children to their mother, Mrs. Balderston, who thanked her again for her careful babysitting. The children delighted Abby and so did the Balderston home; it was so beautiful with its marble floors, four bathrooms, and fitness room. She told Mrs. Balderston how she often told her friends about this house.

Later, she wondered if she had any friends. Why had everyone whispered in the cafeteria and looked so strangely at her later in the corridors?

QUESTIONS FOR DISCUSSION

1. Annie labeled Abby "a liar." This label seemed to travel far and caused Abby to be ignored by her friends. Other than calling Abby a liar, what could Annie have done about the bragging?

2. Jack repeated what he had heard to Ramon. Should he have done so? Why or why not?

3. What were the effects of not talking to Abby? Do such effects help to explain or solve the problem?

4. Abby is unaware of what she did to draw attention to herself. How can this best be handled so that if Abby's behavior needs changing, she knows it?

WRITE ABOUT IT

Neither Annie nor Jack checked on whether Abby was telling the truth. As you think about the story, you decide that it is easy to repeat information you are not really certain is true. List ways you might check on facts, especially facts about people, before you pass them on to someone else.

The Babysitter

Phuong sat looking out the window of the first floor apartment he lived in with his mother, grandfather, and younger brother. It was a warm spring day, and all the kids in his neighborhood were outside playing in the alley. There were three sets of kids playing jump rope, and he stared with envy, wishing he could be there too. But today was Saturday, and his mother had to do the grocery shopping; he knew he would have to watch his kid brother while she was gone. There would be no chance to jump rope today.

This made Phuong sad. He was getting poor marks in school. He still couldn't speak English very well, although his mother made him try every night. Most of the time the other kids wouldn't play with him. Except jump rope. That was different. He had learned to jump rope back in Vietnam. Phuong was fast and quick, and he had a good ear for music, so he could sing the songs and jump all the difficult patterns all at once. He was so nimble and quick that he could do "double-Dutch" faster than any-one else in the neighborhood. The other kids liked to watch him, and it made him feel important. It was the only thing he could do well, and now he had to stay in.

His mother was collecting her things to go out, and she always gave him the same last-minute advice. "Don't leave him alone," she said. "Keep your eyes on him all the time, so he doesn't get into trouble. Give him a snack if he gets hun-gry, and play with him a little bit too."

As she was leaving, his mother took out three pills, put them on a dish in the middle of the kitchen table, and said, "These are Grandpa's pills. When he comes home at lunch time, tell him to be sure to take them. It's very important."

Phuong didn't know exactly what sickness Grandpa had, but he knew it was bad, very bad, because the doctor had said he needed strong medicine. Phuong nodded his head that he had heard her and would do as she said. Then his mother left.

Phuong played with his kid brother, Thanh, for a few minutes, then he turned to the window and stared at all the kids having fun in the alley. They were laughing and screaming and having lots of fun. Whenever someone would step on the rope, everyone else would shout and yell to be sure they knew they were "out." You couldn't get away with anything with this gang. They watched you like a hawk. But that's what made it such fun. You had to be very fast to win.

The more Phuong watched, the worse he felt. Everyone else was having such fun, and he was trapped in the house. Suddenly he got an idea. Why couldn't he just slip out of the house into the alley for a few minutes—maybe just to do one double-Dutch? It would only take three or four minutes, and then he could come right back. He could lock the door so Thanh couldn't get out. He was a good kid; he played with his toys and rode his little tricycle around the kitchen. Perhaps Thanh wouldn't even know that Phuong had left.

The more he thought about it, the bet-ter the idea seemed to be. But then his conscience started to bother him. What if something happened to Thanh while he was gone? His mother would punish him for sure. But what could happen to Thanh? No one could get into the apartment without being seen by the kids jumping rope. Besides Phuong would only be gone a few minutes—not long enough for Thanh to get into trouble.

Phuong finally convinced himself that it would be okay to leave Thanh for a few minutes. He slipped quietly out of the apartment and into the alley outside. The kids greeted him with smiles and offered to let him jump next. It was great. They sang his favorite songs, and he jumped fast and nimbly. He was good, and he knew it. He was having a great time.

"Do it again," cried the kids. So Phuong repeated the whole jump routine. The kids clapped, and Phuong felt good again. Then he realized he had better get back to the apartment and to his kid brother.

He raced into the apartment and looked for Thanh. He wasn't in the bedroom. He wasn't in the living room. Phuong found him in the kitchen, slumped over the tricycle, not moving. He tried to wake his brother, but Thanh didn't respond or move. Phuong was terrified. He started to get that sick feeling in the bottom of his stomach. It was the feeling he got when he knew something bad was going to happen. He loved his kid brother and wouldn't hurt him for anything, but what had happened? What

caused this? How could it have happened in such a short time?

While Phuong was wondering what he should do next, the door opened and his mother entered. She rushed to Thanh and said, "What happened?" She looked at the kitchen table and saw the empty dish where Grandpa's pills had been. Then she turned and looked at Phuong.

QUESTIONS FOR DISCUSSION

1. Were you ever given a responsibility and failed to do it? What were the consequences?

2. Did Phuong's desire to jump rope with the kids justify his leaving his brother alone?

3. Was there a way in which Phuong could have joined the kids for a few minutes and still have watched his brother?

4. It has been said that maturity involves responsibility. Was Phuong acting in a mature way?

WRITE ABOUT IT

Sometimes a task or responsibility can stop us from participating in something we really want to do. We must make a choice. Have you ever faced such a situation? Describe how you acted then and what you would do today if you faced the same choice.

Stopwatch

"I hate him," Andy said to himself. "No matter how hard I try, George always beats me." It was true. Whenever the coach timed the runners, George's time was always faster than Andy's—although generally by just a few seconds.

Ray, Andy's best friend, would just shake his head sadly at the end of each practice session and mutter to Andy, "How does he do it? You practice so hard, Andy."

George walked up next to Ray and looked at Andy with a big grin.

"Knew I'd beat you again, Andy. The best man always wins," he boasted. Then, as he walked away, he turned and shouted, "You know second-best always has to try a bit harder."

Andy tightened his lips to keep from yelling at George or punching him. After a minute, Ray heard him say, "Second-best. I guess that's what I am."

Ray retorted, "No, you're not! He may win races, but he doesn't have any friends. Nobody can stand his boasting."

Still annoyed with himself and with George, Andy replied glumly, "Maybe he has a right to boast."

"No, he doesn't," said Ray. "Everybody's sick of hearing how much he thinks of himself."

As they separated to walk home, Andy said to Ray, "I wish I could win just once. Just once."

Ray thought about Andy on his way home. They had been friends since second grade. Ray, too, would like nothing better than for Andy to win. Maybe George wouldn't be so cocky if Andy beat him just once.

Runners practiced every afternoon. George was always first over the finish line, and Andy was a close second. During these practice sessions, the coach sometimes would hand his stopwatch to a student who wasn't running, and show him how to use the watch and record the time on the clipboard.

The next afternoon, Ray was handed the stopwatch and the clipboard. He recorded George's running time as 8 minutes 7 seconds. Then it was Andy's turn. Ray stood with the watch in his hand and heard George say to someone, "Here comes Mr. Runner-Up. Some people never make it to the top." Ray couldn't stand it. He stopped the watch at 8 minutes 6 seconds for Andy's run and called the time to the coach.

George couldn't believe Andy's time. He yelled at Ray and called him a liar. The coach broke in, scolded George for doubting Ray's time, and reminded him about being a good loser. George went away, grumbling about "stupid time keepers."

Andy, meanwhile, was delighted. This was the very first time he clocked in faster than George. Maybe all those extra weekend runs really had helped. Ray went home feeling mixed up. He felt guilty about what he had done but kept defending himself, saying, "George really is a nerd and, after all, Andy tries so hard, why shouldn't he win at least once?" Despite all his arguments to himself, though, Ray didn't quite feel good about his actions.

QUESTIONS FOR DISCUSSION

1. You are Andy's best friend. Given the stopwatch, what might you have done?
2. What do you think of Ray's actions?
3. Has Ray really helped Andy?
4. If you were Ray, would you tell the coach what you had done? Would you at any time tell Andy? Why?
5. What do you think of George's behavior?
6. George's boasting cost him friends. Yet, he is a very fast runner. How might George be helped to make friends? Would you go to the trouble to help George?

WRITE ABOUT IT

You are the coach, and you are pleased because Andy came in first. You have heard George boast often and know how hurt Andy is about placing second so many times. You also know what close friends Andy and Ray are and find that you are a little suspicious of the timing. Write about how you might handle your suspicions. Would you talk with Ray and Andy? Forget your suspicions? Hereafter keep the stopwatch yourself? What would you do?

The Fire Drill

Li-Fan was happy today. It was the day for the big soccer match between the sixth-grade classes. All the classes had at least one good player, but his class had two, himself and Ernie. Li-Fan knew they had a very good chance to win. He just couldn't wait for the game to take place after school.

Looking at the clock wouldn't make the time pass any faster, so he started reading his textbook assignment for the next day. Suddenly a crazy thing happened! Someone with a ski mask over his face opened the classroom door and yelled, "Fire, fire! Everyone get out as fast as you can!" Then he was gone.

"That's funny," Li-Fan said to himself. "There wasn't any fire bell." All the kids in the room were rushing toward the door. Usually in a fire drill, everyone walked out in a quiet, orderly fashion. He went along with the crowd but, once in the hallway, he saw all the other classes pouring out of their rooms, scrambling and shoving to get to the door.

This was not what they had been told to do. Li-Fan could hear shouts like, "Get out of my way!" and "Move over!" There was a lot of nasty name-calling as everyone tried to get out of the building. Li-Fan went along with the crowd and was soon clear of the building. When he was outside, he noticed there were no fire engines, no firefighters, and no police cars. Something is very strange, he thought. He watched and waited.

After about 15 minutes Mr. King, the principal, appeared. He talked with the teachers for a few moments, and then he spoke to the students on the bullhorn. He said that there was indeed no fire at all. Apparently someone had thought it was a great practical joke to rush into the rooms and yell, "Fire!" The principal was very angry and so were all the teachers. They saw nothing funny in the prank at all.

Oh, well, thought Li-Fan, no harm done, and we even got a little break from the class. Slowly the classes filed back into the building in an orderly fashion as they had been taught.

That's when Li-Fan saw her lying on the floor. It was Megan—one of the first graders. She was lying under the table, unconscious. Li-Fan didn't know her very well, but he did know she had something wrong with her leg and used a crutch to get around. Realizing she was seriously hurt, he hurried to the principal.

"Looks like she was trampled," said the principal. "Tell someone in the office to call the ambulance. We need to get her to the hospital immediately."

As Li-Fan ran to the office, he started thinking again about the fire drill.

Now we have a serious accident, he thought. This isn't funny anymore. He began thinking about the boy in the ski mask. There was something familiar about him. But who was he? Suddenly he remembered seeing someone wear the ski mask, but who? Then remembered. It was Ernie's mask. He was sure of it—there weren't many like that one. It must have been Ernie who pulled the prank.

Suddenly Li-Fan felt sick inside. What a rotten thing to do, he thought. If no one had gotten hurt, it might have been a good joke, but not now with Megan nearly crushed. He might be the only one who knew about Ernie's mask. Should he tell the principal? If he did, Ernie would be punished and certainly taken off the soccer team, and there would go their victory, he thought. But if he didn't identify Ernie, he might do a dumb thing like that again, and someone else would get hurt.

Maybe I'm wrong, thought Li-Fan. Maybe it wasn't Ernie after all. Maybe I should just wait until the principal discovers on his own who did it. By that time, the big game will be over and we will have won. If I say anything now, the game is lost. Li-Fan couldn't decide what to do.

QUESTIONS FOR DISCUSSION

1. Does Li-Fan have a duty to do or say anything to identify the prankster?
2. What would happen if Li-Fan accused Ernie and Ernie had done it?
3. What two factors or thoughts are pulling Li-Fan in opposite directions?
4. Is there any way Li-Fan can get help with this problem?
5. If you were Li-Fan, what would you do?

WRITE ABOUT IT

Pretend you are Li-Fan. Write a letter to a friend and explain the problem. What would be the consequences if you reported Ernie? What if you didn't?

Slam Dunk

As soon as the final school bell had rung, Ahmid grabbed the basketball and raced out the school door for the playground. This was the time of day he liked best. The coach said he was good and Ahmid knew he was right. His body was tall and lean, and he had long legs for running. Coach also said he had good coordination. Ahmid knew he could sink baskets from greater distances than anyone else on the team.

Once on the playground, he dribbled the ball and then started to shoot baskets from different angles, starting close and working farther away each time. Soon his best friend appeared, and he and Chris took turns passing and shooting, trying different angles and distances.

After a short time, three other kids on the team appeared: Josh, Colin, and David. As soon as he had the ball, Ahmid tossed it to Josh and ran close to catch it in return, wanting to include them in the fun. But Josh pivoted around and threw the ball to his friend Colin. Again Ahmid ran close, waiting for an opportunity to catch it, but Colin turned and threw it to David. Ahmid kept trying to get back into the practice, but the other three boys kept the ball exclusively to themselves.

Finally Chris said, "Let's go home. They're not going to let us play at all. Can't you see that? And it's not because we don't play well. We do. It's because we're black. They only let us play when the coach is here and they have to."

Ahmid's stomach was rolling around like a bean in a tin can. "No, no," he yelled, "that's really not so." Inside he knew Chris was right. As they turned to go, the ball suddenly rolled near Ahmid's feet. Quickly he grabbed it, whirled around, and slammed the ball right into the hoop! The other boys watched in amazement as Ahmid retrieved the ball, dribbled around the court, and then made a shot from the other side of the court. Then he turned and deliberately threw the ball to Josh. Josh grabbed it and after taking a few turns at the basket, threw it to Colin, who threw it in turn to David.

Josh, Colin, and David again played with the ball, always keeping it to themselves and never sharing it. This went on for half an hour. "What did you do that for?" shouted Chris. "You know they'll never let us play. They'll always keep it between them. It doesn't matter that you're the best player—we're black, and they're not! They did it to you twice! Don't you get it?

The two friends picked up their school gear and started to walk slowly home. Ahmid was feeling rotten, rotten, rotten! He didn't want to believe what Chris was saying. How could people not like other people for that reason? "Sure, I'm black," he thought, "So what?"

While Ahmid was thinking, Chris was cursing, swearing, and yelling all the bad words he knew—and he knew lots of them. "It just isn't fair, you know," he shouted. "Those guys have no right to act like that to us! We never did anything bad to them! We should think of something real mean and dirty to do back to them! That would fix them."

"I don't think that'll solve the problem," replied Ahmid. "Everyone'll be concentrating on doing bad things to get revenge. Isn't that what's wrong with the world today? No, revenge isn't the answer. We have to think of something better than that."

Ahmid felt he was in over his head on this problem. How do you get people to be fair and not be prejudiced, he won-dered. Ahmid decided that the next day he would talk to the school principal about this. Maybe the principal knew some ways to handle prejudice.

QUESTIONS FOR DISCUSSION

1. Do you think Ahmid and Chris have made an accurate assessment of this situation?

2. Have you ever felt that someone or a group behaved like that to you? How did it make you feel? What did you do about it? Did it work?

3. Pretend you are the principal. What kinds of advice could you offer to these boys?

4. How can you recognize prejudice when you see it?

5. Can one person do anything about it? If so, what?

WRITE ABOUT IT

If you were attending this school, you could write a column for the school newspaper that might help the situation. What would you say?

Flying Eagle

Flying Eagle was his real name. It had been given to him by the tribal council when he and his family lived on the Navaho Reservation. It was a good name, nice and strong, and it always made him think of soaring high above the ground, and being able to fly anywhere. But now his family lived in the town, in a little house, and he no longer dreamed of eagles.

He took the bus each day to the school on the other side of town. The kids didn't like the name, "Flying Eagle," so they had given him the nickname, "F.E." He didn't mind too much because he liked going to school—especially science class. That was cool. Right now they were doing experiments with hamsters. They gave them different kinds of diets and then recorded their weight and growth.

Everyone in class had a hamster and cared for it and recorded its progress. F.E.'s hamster was big, plump, and healthy, so he knew the diet was good for him. Whenever F.E. picked the hamster up, it would cuddle up close to him, almost like it trusted him. F.E. found himself talking to the hamster daily, almost as if it were a child. He really liked the little guy.

One day when the teacher was out of the room, he went to the cage to pick up his hamster. Mike, the biggest boy in the class, yelled loudly, "Hey you, that's my hamster. You leave him alone."

F.E. turned in surprise to see Mike lunging across the room towards him.

"No, this one is mine. I'm certain," said F.E. But it was too late. Mike was across the room in a flash and standing next to F.E. He leaned over and socked him right on the jaw. F.E. fell backwards and hit the corner of the desk.

"A fight, a fight!" yelled the kids. They clambered over one another to get close enough to see it, shouting encouraging comments to both boys.

F.E. didn't want to fight. He had nothing to fight about. He knew the hamster was his because it was the biggest and healthiest one in the class. No matter what Mike thought, he was wrong.

F.E. struggled to his feet and saw Mike waiting for him to respond. Mike really wanted to fight. Then F.E. got mad. It was all Mike's fault. Not only had he made a mistake, but he wanted to take the biggest and best hamster for himself.

F.E. put up his fists and swung at Mike's face. He barely grazed him, while Mike stood there laughing.

"Why don't you learn to fight, Indian?" asked Mike. "Maybe you'd like to use bows and arrows instead?" He smirked, and all the class laughed with him. Just then, one kid yelled, "The teacher, the teacher, she's coming back!"

All the kids scrambled to their seats and, when the teacher entered the room, all was quiet and orderly. F.E. found a paper towel and dabbed at the blood oozing from the cut on his chin. His head

ached from the bump, but most of all he was mad, mad, mad. There was no reason for Mike to do that just because he wanted the best science experiment for himself. F.E. would have shown him the diet he was using on his hamster if Mike had asked him. It wasn't any secret, anyone could have asked. That's what science is all about, F.E. thought. You try different experiments, and see which one works best.

On his way home that afternoon, F.E. suddenly realized that he had forgotten to feed his hamster. With the fight and everything else going on, he was too concerned about other things. He returned quickly to the building, entered the classroom, and fed his hamster. Then he said good night to it, and stroked its fur before carefully putting it back in its cage.

As he started to leave, he was surprised to see Mike entering the classroom. F.E. crouched down behind some tables in the back of the room.

What could he be doing, wondered F.E. He watched closely as Mike went over to the teacher's desk. He had some kind of a tool with him, and he inserted it in the lock of the desk. In a minute or so, the desk opened. Mike reached in and fumbled around inside.

What's he looking for, wondered F.E. There's nothing valuable in there, no money or anything, just the teacher's papers.

Suddenly F.E. remembered. Sometimes the teacher took off her gold watch and kept it in her drawer.

Mike took the watch, quickly locked the desk, and darted out the door.

F.E. knew that if he told people that Mike had stolen the watch, no one would believe him because he lost the fight. They would say that he was just getting back at Mike. F.E. felt sorry for the teacher losing her watch, but he felt a lot worse for himself. He wished Mike would get caught and be punished, but he was sure that wouldn't happen because no one would believe him.

F.E. put his hand into his jacket pocket and pulled out a little envelope. It was the mouse poison his mother had asked him to buy at the store. They'd had trouble with mice in the basement at home, and he was bringing it home to her. Suddenly he got an idea. Mike deserved some punishment, and F.E.

was sure he would never get it. Besides, he owed him one back. Why not give a little of the mouse poison to Mike's hamster? The more he thought about it, the better it sounded.

F.E. looked closely at the package. It was small, but a little would do. He slowly tore open the packet and stood with it in his hands, over Mike's hamster.

QUESTIONS FOR DISCUSSION

1. What would F.E. really accomplish by poisoning Mike's hamster?

2. If you had been F.E., when Mike attacked you, what would you have done?

3. Does F.E. have a responsibility as a member of the class to report the theft of the teacher's watch?

4. When a fight breaks out in a classroom, do the other members of the class have any responsibility for what happens?

5. Do you think F.E. will really poison Mike's hamster? Why or why not?

WRITE ABOUT IT

Does F.E. have the right to injure Mike's hamster? List three arguments supporting this right. List three arguments condemning this right.

Lost Programs?

The music room was always locked when it was not being used. All sorts of instruments and two pianos were housed in the room.

Paolo looked at the locked door and sighed. He had arrived in the United States from Argentina a month ago. In Argentina, he was learning to play the guitar—"guitarra," he called it. His parents had paid for lessons and rented an instrument for him. He really enjoyed playing it and had surprised himself with how well and quickly he learned.

But now Paolo had no guitarra. He had heard his parents talking about how much it was costing them to live in America—more than they had planned on. He just couldn't ask them for money to buy himself a guitar. He kept trying to get up enough nerve to ask Mr. Gunteski, the music teacher, whether there was some way he could borrow an instrument.

Susan was in Paolo's class. She liked him. He was so polite and shy. When she saw him looking at the closed music room door, she said, "It opens right after lunch. You can speak to Mr. Gunteski then."

Paolo was surprised and embarrassed that anyone saw him near the music room and said, "Oh! Oh, that's all right. I don't really need to see Mr. Gunteski." He smiled at Susan and quickly walked away.

Susan's first class after lunch was in the room next to the music room. Several times during the week, she would see Paolo not too far away from the closed

door. She talked with him as they waited for the first class bell. They talked about the school band and the school play and the major events scheduled for field day—an activity Paolo knew nothing about. At one point, Paolo mentioned that he had been learning to play the guitar in Argentina, and he missed playing it since he came to the United States. The class bell stopped further talk.

All the students were surprised when, at the end of the week, the principal called a special assembly for everyone. All the students were guessing what it might mean. A special assembly was rare.

"It must be serious," said one student. "My dad says Mr. Santorio is steaming about something. He's really mad!"

"Wow!" another student interrupted. "Can't wait for this one."

"I can," quipped another. "If it's as bad as they say, I can wait—forever."

Sure enough, when Mr. Santorio began the assembly, he was very serious. He announced that sports equipment had been taken from the supply rooms, and some musical instruments were missing. The police were helping to investigate because so many items had been taken.

"If any one of you can help us with any information, we would appreciate it. We simply don't have enough money to replace the sports equipment and the missing musical instruments. The theft is going to affect the sports program of our school, all our musical events, and even our school play."

Although students left the assembly room silently, they soon began to grumble.

"Boy, I'd like to meet the people who stole our sports equipment. Now I know why we haven't practiced all week."

"I can't take any more violin lessons, Mr. Gunteski just told me. He says most of our string instruments were stolen."

The group became silent as everyone thought about what to do.

Then Gail said eagerly, "Let's be detectives. Does anyone know anything that might help us get the things back?"

Susan sat and thought. She remembered Paolo's frequent visits to the closed music room and his words about missing playing his guitar. She also thought from things he said that his family couldn't afford to buy him an instrument. He had blushed and sort of stuttered when she spoke to him the first day and saw him outside the room. Did that mean he might be guilty of stealing? He was really excited about the sports events, too, when she talked to him about the school schedule. Did he need some equipment to participate?

She really couldn't believe that Paolo was guilty. She heard Gail ask her question again. "Does anyone know anything that might help us get these things back?"

Susan wondered whether the little information she had could "really help." Wouldn't she be putting a doubt in everyone's mind about Paolo? Would she be ruining his reputation?

QUESTIONS FOR DISCUSSION

1. What would you do?

2. Would it be important to find out how Paolo reacted to the news of the theft? How might you find out about this?

3. Should students "play detective"? Is it possible for them to investigate such problems? Can they find the information they need to solve problems like this one?

4. If Susan tells what she knows of Paolo's frequent visits to the closed music room, will Paolo's reputation be hurt? Is his reputation more important than sharing what might help to solve the theft?

WRITE ABOUT IT

Write a note to Paolo telling him what you are thinking about his possible connection in this case. Ask him to explain his frequent visits to the music room.

Art Gone Awry

Lauren was walking towards the school cafeteria thinking about how much fun it was to be in seventh grade. You had different teachers and different subjects. Even lunch time was different. There was a big cafeteria, and you could buy whatever you wanted to eat—no more peanut butter sandwiches in a lunch box. School was really getting to be fun!

Then she met Julie, one of her classmates.

"Hi, Lauren," said Julie. "Why don't you come with me?"

"Where are you going?" asked Lauren.

"Well, it's kind of a secret," Julie said. "You see, the big wall mural we're making in art class is partly finished, and I'm going to work on it now. That'll give us a head start on the work next week."

Lauren thought for a moment, then she asked, "But the room's locked, and we're not supposed to be in there unless the teacher's there. Do you think it's right to go in there alone?"

"Oh, sure," answered Julie. "We won't be doing any harm—just working on the mural. That's a school project, so what's wrong about that?" Then she added, "And I don't think the room's always locked."

Lauren thought for a moment. It sure would be fun to work on the mural alone, without the rest of the class being there, like pretending they were real artists. But then she also knew the rules—nobody in the art room without a teacher.

"Come on," whispered Julie, "don't waste any more time."

The two girls quickly made their way to the art room. The door was closed but not locked. They entered quickly, and no one saw them. Soon they had their paints and brushes and were hard at work.

This is great, thought Lauren. It was another good thing about seventh grade. They got to make their own decisions about what to work on.

They painted away as happy as could be. As they worked, Lauren noticed a large portrait of a woman on the wall next to the mural. There were two American flags on either side of it, and it looked like something important. She realized that the portrait had been done in oil paint and thought that it must have taken someone hours and hours to do that. For a moment, she thought that they should be very careful being so close to that painting. But then Lauren became so interested in doing the mural that she forgot about it.

After half an hour, the bell rang, signaling the end of lunch period. "We'll have to hurry now to get back to class," warned Julie. She jumped off the stool she was standing on and lost her balance. The can of paint she was holding jerked back over her shoulder and splashed all over the oil painting of the woman.

Both girls stared in horror at what had happened. Lauren knew that the portrait had been ruined. Now they would have to go to the principal's office and explain what had happened. They would be punished for being in the art room without permission.

"Let's go and explain to the principal," said Lauren. Julie was calmly wiping off her brushes and preparing to leave. She didn't seem disturbed at all.

"No way," replied Julie. "No one saw us come in, and no one will see us leave. They can't prove we did it. We don't have to tell anyone anything. Just keep quiet, and no one will know."

Lauren was astounded. This was not the way she had been brought up. When she did something wrong, she admitted it and took the punishment—whatever it was. She started to protest, but Julie was ready to leave. Their next class was ready to start. She walked silently along beside Julie, but somehow everything had gone sour. She didn't feel good about school at all now. This wasn't right.

About an hour later, the principal came into the classroom. He spoke to the teacher for a few minutes and then to the class. He looked very serious and sad.

"Boys and girls," he said. Something very sad has happened. We had a wonderful principal at this school for 30 years. Everyone loved her because she was so good to all the children. A portrait of her painted by a famous artist was in the art room. Something has happened to

it. There's paint all over it. We don't know if it was an accident or if it was deliberate. Do any of you know what happened?"

The students in the class looked shocked, but no one said a word. The principal waited a few moments, looking intently at each one of the students. Still no one moved. "Were any of you in the art room today?" he asked. "If so, we might be able to determine the time when it happened."

Lauren stole a quick glance at Julie. Surely she would tell the principal what had happened—how they had gone in just to work, and it had happened by accident. Julie just sat there without saying anything. Lauren was squirming in her seat—surely she must look guilty. The principal asked everyone to let him know if they found any information about the accident, and then he left.

The rest of the day was a nightmare for Lauren. She couldn't concentrate on her classes. She couldn't look at Julie. She

decided that since Julie had wrecked the painting, it was her problem. Julie should go to the principal and confess. After school Lauren tried to talk to Julie but she had left school fast and wasn't anywhere to be found.

When she got home, Lauren threw herself on her bed. It was all Julie's fault, she reasoned. Julie had gotten her to go to the art room in the first place. Julie is lying, she thought, by not admitting it. As she thought about it some more, Lauren realized that she, too, was lying by not responding to the principal's questions. This made her feel worse. She was guilty of lying, even if she hadn't ruined the painting.

QUESTIONS FOR DISCUSSION

1. Does it make any difference who spilled the paint since the painting is already ruined?

2. Should Lauren say she spilled the paint to protect a friend?

3. Is Julie really a good friend?

4. What should Lauren do? If she told the principal what had happened, it would implicate her friend. If she didn't tell, she would be lying.

WRITE ABOUT IT

Help Lauren straighten out her own thinking. Make two columns: List reasons why Lauren should tell the principal in one column and list reasons why Lauren should not tell the principal in the other column. Which list do you agree with?

No Limit on Wit

"The play's the thing," the sixth-grade teacher kept saying.

It sure is, thought Debby. If you aren't in it, you just aren't anything or anyone.

For years she had done all kinds of behind-the-scene jobs. Her brothers teased her about being the most important stage "ghost." So did her father but he said, with a smile of pride, that the little kids couldn't do without her. Reluctantly she admitted that the teachers always said how helpful she was. A little in-front-of-the-curtain responsibility would be nice, though.

Each year the school planned a production involving all the students. Everybody in school participated in some way. Everybody at home participated too; they were the audience. The whole town, or at least most of it, attended the play and cheered the players.

It was exciting, Debby had to admit. Everyone seemed so proud of their children, their school, and even their town. She thought she, too, should be proud but instead was annoyed, even angered, at being asked every year to do the "usual thing"—organize the younger children behind the curtain and help adults ready them for their various performances.

Debby listened as Steve and Latoya talked about how Danny could possibly participate. "What could a cripple do?" asked Steve. "He'll look weird in the line of kids in costumes. Besides, we'll have to get

a ramp pushed in each time he has to practice on stage." Steve, who was doing his "usual"—managing some of the production needs—was annoyed at the extra work that accommodating Danny would involve.

Debby could understand why Steve was angry about his assignment, but she was uncomfortable with the way he talked about Danny.

Danny was a wit. He was the funniest kid in her class. He seemed to be the life of class discussions and at ease with his wheelchair. It was because of Danny's ready wit that this year, for the first time, he was scheduled to participate onstage in the annual production. He had been assigned a part that called for quick, witty answers. Wit was so characteristic of Danny that everyone agreed that he should be cast in the part. Debby was delighted when she heard. She thought this would show Danny how much he was appreciated.

Turning to go to the back of the auditorium, she was surprised to see Danny quite close by and even more surprised to see an unhappy expression on his face. She suddenly realized that Danny had probably heard Steve's remarks.

Debby walked over to Danny and smiled at him. He didn't respond with his usual bright glance. Still she stopped to chat with him before reporting to Mrs. Chen, the third grade teacher who was assembling her students. Debby felt badly for Danny and decided to tell Steve that his comments were thoughtless and unkind. As she thought about scolding Steve, however, she realized that this might not really help Danny or Steve understand how much they each were appreciated. How could she help accomplish that, she wondered.

Debby waited until the night of the final production. She knew Danny had to be backstage early so that when the curtain opened he would be center stage. She decided to talk to him and ask him to make a few jokes about how hard the production crew worked. When she talked with Danny, his mind started running in its usual ticker-tape fashion. He grinned at her and said, "Sure. You mean like, 'Hey, folks, you know we got magicians here? When this production crew gets going and Steve writes his orders on the board, he puts magic in his magic markers. That's why this wheelchair is stage center and why you are now going to be entertained by that famous "Wheelchair Wit"—namely me.'"

Debby laughed. She'd never stop being amazed at Danny. "You are the funniest!" she told him, grinning. As she walked away, she wondered if the teachers would be disturbed by Danny's introducing some jokes of his own—ad libs—she heard Miss D'Angelo call them. She didn't think so.

Danny was rare, Debby thought again. He was really happy about entertaining others. He didn't go around feeling sorry for himself, and he hadn't let Steve get to him.

After the show Debby realized that if she hadn't been doing her "usual thing" in the auditorium, she would not have heard Steve's remarks and, therefore, could have given no thought about how to deal with them.

QUESTIONS FOR DISCUSSION

1. Debby did not scold Steve for his comments. What would you have done?

2. Steve actually was to receive praise rather than punishment for his behavior. What do you think about this?

3. What do you think about Debby's handling of this situation?

4. If you were Steve, what would you do after the final production, after hearing Danny praise you?

WRITE ABOUT IT

Write a paragraph that suggests ways your school could change to be sure disabled students are able to participate in school activities.

Raising the Hoop

Ben had an important job to do. He was wearing his black sweatshirt, black pants, and a black woolen cap. Black things don't show up well at night, he knew, so he was prepared. He made his way slowly into the school gym through an open window, and now he was prepared to do his job.

Ben was the forward on the high school basketball team. Basketball was everything to him. He was good at it, and it gave him a feeling of being important when all the students in the bleachers and stands would clap and shout for him.

His team just had to win. It meant everything to him. This game tomorrow night was a problem. The visiting team from Easton High was good, real good. Their forward was even taller than Ben, and that meant the visiting team would probably get most of the first jumps, giving their team a big advantage.

That's when Ben thought of his idea. If he raised the level of the basketball hoop just three inches, it would throw them all off-balance. They wouldn't know what hit them. Of course, he would have to be careful to repaint the backboard so no one would notice the change. The fans wouldn't see the small change from their seats, and the players would be too busy to notice.

Ben knew that usually the two sides exchanged baskets at half time, but the referee they would have tomorrow didn't usually bother to do that. The visitors could have the higher basket for both halves of the game. His own team wouldn't have it at all.

Ben had a lot of work to do. Quietly and slowly, he removed the basketball hoop from its place on the backboard and raised it up three inches. Then he carefully put putty in the old holes and repainted them to resemble the remainder of the board. He gazed at it with a pleased, satisfied look. It hardly showed at all.

No one would ever know unless they examined it very closely, thought Ben. He felt satisfied that he had done a good job.

He carefully swept the floor underneath the basket so there were no pieces of putty left to cause suspicion, then he gathered together his equipment, and quietly left the gym.

The next night was the big game. The gym was crowded. The bleachers were packed with the students and their families. This will be a great game, thought Ben.

The first half went well. The game was fast and exciting as the players raced back and forth across the court. The home team made 18 baskets quite easily, but the visitors had trouble. They were a good team, and all the players worked hard, but every time they made a shot they missed. Only six shots got in. Their players looked discouraged and puzzled. Usually their shots succeeded—real dunkins. They tried harder and harder.

Ben was delighted. His scheme was working. The referee blew the whistle for the second half to begin. Ben took his position to jump for the ball but suddenly the referee said, "Change sides." Ben couldn't believe his ears. This referee had never bothered to do that before. Ben stood still and looked at the referee with horror. If they changed sides, his team would get the high basket. His whole plan would be ruined!

"Move, move," said the referee, and he motioned for Ben to change sides. There was nothing he could do. Ben changed sides, and the whole second half of the game was a disaster. The situation was reversed. The visiting team made all their baskets, and his home team missed most of theirs. The final score was 52-50 in favor of the visiting team. Ben said nothing but, when he went home to bed, he couldn't sleep at all. His mind was whirling with questions. His scheme had failed. Would his team have won if he hadn't moved the basketball hoop? Should he replace the basketball hoop at the correct height? What would his teammates think if they knew what he had done?

QUESTIONS FOR DISCUSSION

1. What was basically wrong about Ben's scheme?

2. When is an action right or wrong? How do we know?

3. Were other people hurt by Ben's scheme? Who?

4. If he told the coach about his action, what would be the consequences?

5. If he didn't tell the coach, what would be the consequences?

6. Many people get tempted to do wrong things. How can we keep them from doing these things?

WRITE ABOUT IT

Did you ever think of doing something that was "wrong" just to win a game? Write a story about yourself, using another name, and tell what you planned to do and whether or not you actually did it.

The White Stuff

Tod was feeling rotten, rotten, rotten! Everything had gone wrong in the last few weeks. First, he failed the big math test, which meant that he would have to take the course again in summer school. That would ruin his summer—his only time to play and have fun. Then he didn't do all of his English homework last week, so his parents grounded him for 10 days. That meant Tod had to go directly home after school and couldn't play with the other boys, or go anywhere else. That was a big bore. Then, he had tried out for the basketball team for next year and was rejected. He hadn't even made the first cut. It was just no fun being at the bottom of the pile in everything.

Tod saw his friend Mike in the boys' room and was surprised when he saw Mike pull a little glass vial from his pocket, open it, and pour some white stuff that looked like pebbles into a little pipe. Then Mike proceeded to light it.

"Hi, Mike," said Tod. "What's up?"

Mike looked startled. He put out the pipe and stuffed it into his pocket. They talked about the new basketball team and the fact that Mike had been accepted on the team for next year. Tod congratulated Mike on making it and said he was sorry and angry that he didn't get on it also. "It's been a pretty bad time for me all around," said Tod, and he told Mike about the other problems too. Mike was very sympathetic and said he would help him in any way he could, but neither of the boys quite knew what to do.

Suddenly Mike reached into his pocket and pulled out the vial again, poured some more pebbles into the pipe, and lit it. Then he held it out to Tod and said, "Well, you could try this. It'll really make you feel better."

"What is it?" asked Tod.

"Well, it's something that makes you feel really great. Just try it," replied Mike. "I use it all the time."

Tod looked carefully at the pipe and said, "Where did you get this stuff?" Mike said, "You just buy it yourself." Something inside Tod made him hesitate. He handed the pipe back to Mike. "No, but thanks anyway."

For the next three days, Mike offered Tod the pipe each day, and Tod refused each time. Then on the fourth day, when they met again, Tod started thinking about how Mike had said it made you feel so good. Mike certainly looked good and seemed to feel good all the time. After all, Mike had made the team and Tod hadn't. Mike always seemed to do the right thing.

He never got into trouble. If Mike was using the white stuff, it couldn't be too bad. Whatever it was, it was doing a good job for Mike. Tod thought maybe he could try it just once to see how it worked. Just once wouldn't hurt.

The next time it was offered to him, Tod accepted the pipe and smoked it. Nothing happened for a while, but then he suddenly started feeling very good about himself, about school, and even about being grounded. He ran around the court and shot baskets for an hour, feeling as if he could beat a whole team all by himself. This was great stuff, he thought. I feel so much better—the other things don't really matter at all.

That night it was well past midnight before Tod could get to sleep. His mind was racing. The next morning it was a very different story. He could hardly get up; he was so tired he couldn't eat break-fast. His mother looked at him strangely but said nothing.

When Tod got to school, he told Mike what had happened, that he felt great at first but now he felt worse than ever. Mike told him that he just needed another "hit," and he offered the pipe to him right away. Tod took it gratefully. The same thing happened for the next five days. Then when Tod asked Mike for another "hit," Mike said, "O.K. but this time it'll cost you. You have to pay for it."

"Pay for it?" asked Tod. "What do you mean pay for it?"

"From now on," replied Mike, "It'll cost you two dollars for each vial."

"But I don't have two dollars," com-plained Tod. "I only have 50 cents left from my allowance last week, and I won't get anymore until next week."

"Sorry. No money, no vial," shrugged Mike. "That's the way it is." He walked away without even a glance behind him.

Tod felt miserable. Smoking the pipe had made him feel so good at first, but now he felt worse than ever—even worse than before he started smoking the pipe. Mike obviously wasn't going to give him any more without the money. That was for sure. He had no money and no way to get any, either. Then Tod thought about his mother's grocery money. He knew where she kept it, but he dropped that idea because he knew she would find out. Tod didn't know which way to turn. He felt so awful. His head ached, everything ached. Bones he never knew he had were aching. He just had to get another "hit." What should he do?

QUESTIONS FOR DISCUSSION

1. What do you think the white stuff was?

2. Why does Tod feel so badly after feeling so good?

3. What was happening to Tod? Do you think he realizes this?

4. Was Mike a friend or not?

5. What would be the best thing for Tod to do now?

6. If Tod steals money this week, what will happen next week?

WRITE ABOUT IT

Pretend you are Tod's friend. He tells you his problem. Write a letter to him giving him advice about his problem.

The Contract

Ling and Liu were the only two Asian students in Washington School. They had left China to come to America because their father said there was more opportunity here for people who wanted to work hard. Their father wanted his children to have the chance for more education than he had had. He rented a small grocery store and sold groceries to people in the neighborhood.

Their mother and father worked long hours to keep the store up-to-date and clean. Ling also was expected to do a major share of the work in the store. Every day after school, he ran home and went to work in the back room of the store, sorting vegetables and cleaning the vegetable bins so they would look attractive to the customers. His sister, Liu, helped too, waiting on customers and packaging the groceries.

There was another small room in the store, behind the back room. This was where the family lived. By American standards, it was a small room for a whole family to live in, but compared to their former place in China, it was large.

The only sad part for Ling was that he was so busy between school and the store he had no time to see other things. There was so much about this new country he wanted to see, but he felt it would be years before he would be able to go places—the Statue of Liberty, the Empire State Building, the Grand Canyon—all those famous places.

Then one day in history class, Miss Foy, the teacher made a wonderful announcement. She said the class was going to go on a field trip to the state museum. All the students shouted, "Yay, yay!" Then Miss Foy announced that everyone in the class would help with the planning. Someone would arrange the date with the museum, a transportation committee would arrange for a bus, someone would arrange for lunches, and so forth. Everyone started to call out what he or she wanted to do.

Ling said nothing. He was delighted to be going on the trip during school time because he knew his parents would approve that. It was also a way for him to see other places. Miss Foy had told the class that the state museum had wonderful exhibits of dinosaurs, whales, and all kinds of unusual animals. There was also an art gallery. It sounded like a wonderful place to visit.

Suddenly Miss Foy said, "No one signed up to arrange for the transportation, and I see Ling hasn't chosen anything either, so Ling, you will be in charge of the transportation." Ling didn't mind. His English wasn't perfect, but it was pretty good. He thought he could handle the job.

For the next few days, Ling was pretty busy. He consulted the yellow pages in the telephone book to locate the bus companies and to ask the fees for driving the class to the museum. When they heard his accent on the phone, some companies just hung up the receiver and didn't even let him finish his conversations. Ling was upset by their rudeness, but he kept trying.

Finally, he located a bus company several towns away. Ling described the job of driving the class to the museum in the morning and back again late in the afternoon. The Blue Bus Company quoted a price which seemed fair to Ling, and so he set the date. They wanted a deposit to seal the agreement.

Ling informed Miss Foy of the arrangement, and she seemed pleased. She wrote her own personal check to pay for the deposit. The class members would contribute their share later.

The next day Ling reported the results of his work to the class. Everyone seemed pleased. Each day, someone else spoke about what he or she had arranged. The whole class was eager and ready to go. Some of the kids were talking about what they were going to wear; everyone was hoping it wouldn't rain. They found out they could bring brown-bag lunches and buy drinks in the museum's cafeteria. That helped to reduce the cost for everyone. Kids who had cameras made sure they had film to take along. It promised to be a wonderful trip, and most of the kids could hardly wait.

The day of the trip finally arrived. All the students were in front of the school a half hour before the bus was scheduled to arrive. Everyone had on their best clothes. For a while, they talked about what they were going to see, but as the time drew near for the bus to arrive, a sudden quietness fell over the group. They were really going somewhere special, and they felt very grown up and important.

As the clock on the school wall ticked past the departing time, the students started to get worried. "Do you suppose they forgot about us?" someone asked.

"Maybe the driver doesn't know the way to the school?"

"Are you sure you told them the right date?"

All these questions kept coming at Ling since he was in charge of the transportation.

After waiting another half hour, Miss Foy and Ling went to the principal's office to call the Blue Bus Company. Miss Foy telephoned, and Ling could tell by watching her face that it was bad news. She put down the receiver slowly and looked sadly at Ling.

"They've gone out of business," she said sadly, as if she really couldn't believe it herself.

"But that can't be," said Ling. "They accepted your check and arranged for the date."

"I'm afraid it's true," answered Miss Foy. "I hate to have to tell the class. They'll be so disappointed."

"It's my fault 'cause I made the arrangements," said Ling. "I should tell them."

He went outside very slowly. He reported the results of the telephone call by Miss Foy to the bus company. The kids looked at him in disbelief. They just couldn't believe it—their whole day ruined. Their fun all destroyed, no museum, nothing!

Then the nasty remarks started.

"It's your fault, Ling. Why didn't you do it right?"

"Why didn't you check out the company before you gave them our money?"

"When you made the deal did you speak to them in Chinese? Why didn't you speak English?"

"We should have known better than to trust someone like you with our money."

At that point, Miss Foy came out. The nasty remarks stopped. She motioned for them all to enter the school building for a regular school day. As the class filed past Ling, there were more dirty looks and nasty remarks.

QUESTIONS FOR DISCUSSION

1. Pretend you're Ling. Argue for yourself. Defend your actions.

2. Is the class right in assigning blame to Ling?

3. Is there another person who should assume part of the responsibility?

4. What steps could Ling have taken to prevent this from happening?

5. Did being Chinese have anything to do with this problem? Why or why not?

WRITE ABOUT IT

Ling's experience has happened to other people. Talk to any person who runs a business. Ask him or her to tell you what legal steps Ling and the school could take to get their money back. Then create a "consumer awareness" brochure that details your findings.

Silent Witness

There were many Vietnamese families moving into the area around Valley School, and that meant their children would be attending school there. Soon people began to notice that many of the Vietnamese kids worked very hard, not only outside school but also inside. They always had their homework done on time and their papers ready, and they studied for every test as if it were the last one in the world. Soon it became evident that they were getting the highest marks in school, too. The kids who used to be first in some classes lost their places to Vietnamese students, and they now became third or fourth. Some people, like Brad, didn't like this.

Brad had had the highest record in his class for the last two years, but now he had some close competition. He didn't like that. He didn't like it at all. Whenever he had a chance, Brad would make some ugly comment, like "Why don't they go back where they belong?" It didn't matter to him that most of these families had lost everything before they came here, or that their villages and their homes had been destroyed.

It's not my fault, thought Brad. Why should they come here and ruin everything for me?

The last day of school was coming up soon, and the principal would be announcing the highest ranked student in each class. Brad wanted that with all his heart. He'd had it before, and he felt it really belonged to him. He deserved it. Recently he had been watching Bao, a Vietnamese kid in his class. His test marks were always high, and Brad was afraid that Bao was getting close to him—maybe even passing him. It's not right, thought Brad. I shouldn't be beaten in my own school by an outsider.

Then there was Jill. Brad got even madder when he thought of her. She wasn't his girl, that is not really. But she always smiled at him when he saw her, and she even skated with him at the rink—that was real fun, skating together. Now she was smiling at Bao too—not just in a friendly way but in a way that said she liked him. They even talked together a lot. Brad couldn't understand why she would prefer Bao over him.

Bao could sense the hostility and hate developing more each week. He knew Brad had been the top-ranked student the year before. What could he do? Should he pretend to be dumb just to please Brad? He needed the good marks to get ahead. His parents had warned him about that. They knew he would face jealousy and resentment in a new country, but that it was his duty to get a good education. That way he could get a better job to earn more money to bring his aunt, uncle, and cousins over.

Then one day Brad was walking closely behind Bao in the hall. Too closely, Bao thought, but he kept going. Suddenly Bao found himself on the floor. Brad had tripped him. Bao swung around, jumped up, and started to swing at Brad. Then he stopped. There was enough bad feeling between them now—no use increasing it. As Brad stood there grinning, Bao stared hard at him and walked on.

"Coward, coward," called Brad. Bao walked on, out of earshot.

The next week Brad got an idea. He decided he'd show Bao whose girl Jill was. He wanted to prove that she liked him.

It was late Friday afternoon. Most of the students had left, so the building was almost deserted. Brad knew Jill was staying late to finish her special project in the library and that she would be coming down the hall soon. He waited quietly inside the book closet until she appeared. Then he jumped out, grabbed her from behind, and pushed her into the closet. Closing the door behind him, he threw his arms around her and kissed her hard on the lips.

"Stop, stop," Jill shouted. "What are you doing? Let go of me!" Brad only held her tighter. He kept kissing her and hugging her for several minutes. She pushed and pulled at him, but it was no use. He was much stronger. Finally she gave a final lunge, pushed Brad away, and got out the door.

Bao had stayed late that night too, and he was at the other end of the corridor, just leaving, when he saw Jill burst out of the closet and run to the principal's office. He knew something was wrong. Soon he saw Brad emerge from the closet and run out of the building.

Bao walked closer to the principal's office, and he could soon hear Jill half crying, half yelling, "It was Brad! I know it! I saw him!"

"Brad's always been a responsible student. This doesn't sound like something he would do," said the principal. "Did anybody else see this?" continued the principal. "Were there any witnesses?"

"Of course not," yelled Jill. "He wouldn't have done it if anybody was around."

Jill and the principal went on talking. Bao listened and wondered what to do.

If he told the principal he had seen Brad come out of the closet after Jill left, he would be a witness. That would prove Brad was guilty. Brad would certainly make it very tough for him. If he remained quiet and didn't tell what he saw, no one would believe Jill. They might just say she had imagined it.

What if people said he was lying because he wanted to get even with Brad? What if Brad was proven guilty? He might be expelled from school, and that would be less competition for the No. 1 position.

Bao knew he had to either go into the principal's office and tell what he saw, or else get out of there fast and keep silent. What should he do?

QUESTIONS FOR DISCUSSION

1. If you were Bao, what reasons might you give for going home and saying nothing?

2. List reasons you might give for telling the principal what you know.

3. Have you ever witnessed something and then not told about it? Was the consequence of your decision good or bad?

4. Does Bao owe anything to Jill? Why should he get involved?

5. Has fear ever kept you from doing something you knew was right to to?

WRITE ABOUT IT

Bao will probably tell his mother what happened today at school. If you were his mother, what would you advise him to do? Why? Write a paragraph explaining what you would tell him.

How Do You Say, "No"?

Gina liked chorus in school. She had a sweet soprano voice and good pitch and, whenever there was a solo part in one of the pieces, Ms. Glass gave her the part. That made her rather special because all the kids got to know her name and who she was. It made her feel very important. Now the boys noticed her and would smile as she passed. Gina liked this new feeling of popularity. Some of the boys would now come over to talk to her before and after the rehearsals, and that was great. Sometimes there would be three or four boys talking to her all at once. They joked, kidded each other, and told funny stories. It was cool!

There was one special boy, Sam. He was older than the others because he had to repeat a grade. He was bigger and taller and even had a little beard, which made him look handsome. His white teeth flashed every time he grinned. Somehow Gina felt very attracted to him. She felt so special when he smiled at her—all warm and happy inside.

One day, Ms. Glass decided to move the sections of the chorus around. Instead of having the sopranos and altos sit together and the tenors and basses sit together, she decided to have the sopranos sit next to the tenors and the altos next to the basses. Gina didn't much care where anyone sat, as long as she could sing and get some solo parts. Since Sam was a tenor, he sat next to her group and,

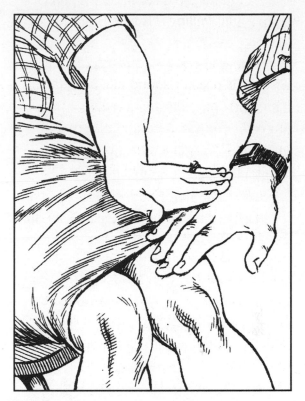

to her surprise, Sam pushed right into the row where she was so he could sit right beside her.

Gina smiled when she saw him and was flattered that he wanted to be near her. Sam gave her his big smile, and it made Gina very happy. The rehearsal started, and soon they were all involved in the music. There was a small solo part for Gina and, when it was her turn to sing, she stood up and sang. She knew she had done well, whether anybody told her so or not. She had practiced and worked very hard on that one song.

When it was over she looked at Sam expecting to see him smile. Instead he reached over and patted her leg. Then he moved his hand under her skirt. Gina was shocked. She pushed his hand away. Sam became angry and turned away from her.

The next time chorus met for rehearsal, Sam was beside her again in the next seat. This time Gina didn't smile at him or even speak to him, but he didn't seem to mind. Again the same thing happened. Sam put his hand on her leg and moved it up under her skirt. This time, Gina looked directly at him as she removed his hand and said, "Sam, please don't do that."

Sam made no response at all—just as if Gina had said nothing. Twice again during the rehearsal, he did it, but each time Gina moved his hand off.

Before the next rehearsal started, Gina made certain that it wouldn't happen again. She found two girlfriends sitting together and asked if she could sit between them. Now that Gina was so popular, they were glad to agree. They separated and let Gina sit between them. She was sure this would prevent Sam from sitting beside her.

When Sam entered the room, his eyes searched for Gina, and he looked angry when he found her sitting between the girls. His face was mean and determined as he walked over to them.

"You're sitting in my seat," he growled at one of the girls. "Go find yourself another one." He pulled one girl up by her arm and moved her out of the seat. Then he plopped himself into the seat beside Gina.

Gina liked being popular with the boys. It was fun, and it made her feel good. Maybe she should let Sam touch her. After all, no one could see him. No one would know. She really didn't like the whole idea. She knew she needed to talk to someone, but who? Gina hated to admit that anyone had tried that on her. It made her feel bad. She wondered if other girls let boys do this. She wondered whether girls had to let it happen so they could be popular.

QUESTIONS FOR DISCUSSION

1. Sam continues to annoy Gina even though Gina has asked him not to. What should Gina do about this situation? Should she get advice from someone? If so, who?

2. Do girls have to do things they don't feel comfortable with to be popular?

3. When a boy harasses a girl, what rights does she have to stop it?

4. Does the opposite situation, a girl harassing a boy, ever happen? Would you treat it the same way?

WRITE ABOUT IT

Do girls ever annoy boys in some embarrassing way? What do they do? How do boys feel about it?

The Softball Team

Cori was happy. Spring was here, and her school had two softball teams, the Gold and the Blue. Softball was her favorite sport, and each year they had wonderful games. Best of all, she had been elected captain of the Gold team, and that made her special. Everyone knew who she was, and it made her feel like she was really somebody important.

All the girls on the team worked hard at the three practice sessions each week. They worked on hitting, catching, pitching, and running around the school grounds to build stamina. Best of all, there was a good feeling among the teammates. They all got along well together. Cori thought it was because whenever there was an issue or problem she had them vote, and then they did what the majority wanted. It was like a democracy, she thought. So everything was going just fine.

Then it happened. At practice one afternoon, Cori looked up to see the coach coming onto the mound. Walking beside her was the smallest person Cori had ever seen. Her head only came up to the coach's belt.

Coach acted very casually as if there was nothing unusual, but Cori knew very well that this was something different. Cori knew that every girl on the team was watching what was happening.

"Girls," said the coach, "this is Maggie. She's new. I know that you will make her feel welcome."

As captain of the team, Cori knew she had to act for the group, so she shook hands with the new girl and tried hard to smile. She made small talk with her asking about where she used to live and what it was like there. She knew every eye was watching them. The other girls were as surprised as she was. After a few minutes, Cori suggested they start a practice game. As the girls prepared to begin, lots of strange thoughts ran through Cori's head.

They had never had a situation like this before. The school rule was that the softball teams were open to everyone; there could be no rejections. They always had welcomed new girls, but this was different. Could she hit? Could she pitch? Could she catch? How would she get along with all the others? Would this spoil all the fun they now had?

About this time, it was Maggie's turn at bat. She walked slowly up to the plate and stood ready. Every eye in the group was on her. The pitcher threw a nice steady low ball. Maggie swung her bat and smacked the ball—a really good hit. It sailed over the field into the outfield. Everyone started to yell, "Yay, yay." It was almost a chant. For a moment, Cori felt a sigh of relief. Maybe this wasn't going to be so bad after all. Maybe there wouldn't be a problem. Maybe things would work out.

The tension in Cori's stomach started to break, and her hands stopped sweating—but only for a moment. After Maggie hit the ball, she dropped the bat and started to run to first base. Then Cori saw the problem. The second base player ran for the ball, caught it, and threw it like lightning to the first base. Although Maggie ran as fast as she could, she was no match for the swift ball, and she was quickly tagged out.

The other teammates saw this, too, and knew exactly what it meant. There was dead silence. No one said anything. Soon the practice was over, but Cori knew she would be hearing from the girls. She did. That night after supper, they came over to her house to discuss the problem. Everyone had something to say.

"We just can't have her on our team," said Kim.

"You know what'll happen," agreed Liz. "She may be able to hit, but she can't run. It isn't her fault. She just can't do it."

"Every time she gets up to bat, she'll make an out for sure," added Latifah. "No matter how good she hits, it won't matter."

"We have to think of the good of the whole team," continued Liz. "We'll never win with her on the team. It just isn't fair to the rest of us."

Cori argued with them. "Why not give her a chance and see what happens? You know the rule. There are no rejections." The rest of the team was adamant.

Cori knew that the team expected her to put this to a vote, just as they always had done. She argued for a while longer, trying to persuade them to wait and try it first, but finally she agreed to vote. It was unanimous—they all wanted to get Maggie off the team. The team members left. Cori went to bed, but she couldn't sleep. So many troubled thoughts kept whirling around in her mind.

Was it always like this for Maggie? How did she get on and off chairs? How did she reach things on high shelves or get up very steep steps? Did everyone reject her like this? Did everyone act as if she were strange and different?

How would I feel if I were a dwarf like Maggie, wondered Cori. What should I do tomorrow? If I report the team vote to the coach, what will happen? Would the coach break the rule? Is there anything else I can do? Maybe I shouldn't have let the team vote on this.

QUESTIONS FOR DISCUSSION

1. Did you ever stand up for something you knew was right? What happened?

2. Have you ever found yourself thinking differently from the group? Did you change or keep your ideas?

3. Is there any compromise Cori can make in this situation?

4. Is it sometimes right to break a rule? When? How?

WRITE ABOUT IT

Do you think your school should have rules or a policy about including or excluding students from school teams? Write a set of rules or a policy you think your school could use.

Suggestions for Further Reading and Discussion

Tuck Everlasting
Babbitt, Natalie
Farrar, Straus and Giroux
1975

In the book *Tuck Everlasting*, 10-year-old Winnie Foster finds a magic spring. Anyone who drinks from the spring lives forever. When members of the Tuck family who have sampled the spring find that Winnie knows the secret of the spring, they worry about her and later kidnap her to explain the seriousness of her discovery.

Invite your students to think about and discuss:
- the behavior of the Tucks. Why did the Tucks kidnap Winnie?
- why Mae Tuck killed the yellow-suited man.
- why Winnie made the choice she did.

Ask your students what choice they would have made.

The King's Fountain*
Alexander, Lloyd
Illustrated by Ezra Jack Keats
Dutton
1975

In *The King's Fountain*, a poor man fearfully visits the King to plead with him to forget his plan to build a fountain on castle grounds. Such a fountain would divert water away from all his subjects.

Invite your students to think about and discuss:
- why the poor man was so fearful.
- why all the persons he asked to deliver the message to the King appear in the end to be unfit for the task.
- the illustrations and whether they help the reader to understand the poor man's dilemma.

Ask your students what they would have done if they were the poor man or the king.

Homecoming
Voigt, Cynthia
Atheneum
1981

In *Homecoming*, Dicey Tillerman leads her younger sister and two young brothers from Connecticut to Maryland in search of a grandmother they have never met. Abandoned by their mother and father, the Tillerman children want to stay together. Since they have no money and no home, separation into foster homes is a very real possibility.

Invite your students to think about and discuss:
- the fact that Dicey lies and steals on her way to Maryland.
- why Dicey lied.
- what else Dicey might have done to keep the family together.

*Out of print, but readily available in most libraries.

Ask your students what they would have done if they were faced with Dicey's dilemma.

Racing the Sun
Pitts, Paul
Avon
1988

Twelve-year-old Brandon Rogers is embarrassed to introduce his Navaho Indian grandfather to his friends. Brandon ignores his grandfather when they see each other in a mall, and he has some strong reactions to this later.

Invite your students to think about and discuss:
* times they were embarrassed about family members or friends.
* why Brandon behaved the way he did.
* why Brandon was extremely upset later.
* the part father played in Brandon's behavior.

Ask your students what they might have done in Brandon's place.

Shiloh
Naylor, Phyllis Reynolds
Atheneum
1991

Eleven-year-old Marty Preston finds a mistreated beagle he names Shiloh. He works hard to protect and later to own Shiloh. Early on, Marty hides Shiloh from his cruel owner but is found out and compelled by his father to return the dog. Marty is confused and doesn't understand the need to return the dog to pain. Right and wrong seem to be all mixed up.

Invite your students to think about and discuss:
* why Marty was confused about what to do about Shiloh.
* the fact that Marty was troubled about lying, yet he did lie. Why?
* why Marty obeyed Judd Travers even though he was an impossible boss. Were there other ways Marty might have become the owner of Shiloh? If so, why did he choose the most difficult one?

Ask your students what they would have done in Marty's place.

A Place to Claim as Home*
Willis, Patricia
Clarion
1991

In *A Place to Claim as Home*, 13-year-old Henry Compton, an orphan, is hired to do summer work on Sarah Morrison's farm in Ohio when older workers leave to join the armed forces during World War II. Henry has no special liking for a neighborhood boy, Evan, but, when Evan falls into a mine shaft and is trapped, Henry edges his way down the shaft to join Evan until they are rescued. They suffer a cave-in but eventually free themselves.

Invite your students to think about and discuss:
* Henry's decision to join Evan in a dark mine shaft in which he too might be trapped.

*Out of print, but readily available in most libraries.

• other ways Henry might have helped Evan.

Ask your students what they would have done if they were Henry.

Sam, Bangs and Moonshine
Ness, Evaline
Holt, Rinehart and Winston
1966

Samantha, called Sam for short, invents tales often about her mother who died years ago. Among the tales Sam invents are ones about owning a lion and baby kangaroo and having a mother who was a mermaid. Tommy, Sam's friend, believes all of Sam's tales but Bangs, Sam's cat, doesn't. Sam's father called her tales "moonshine" and cautioned her to stop spreading them. Sam is disobedient, and her disobedience creates major problems.

Invite your students to think about and discuss:
• why Sam invents stories.
• what Sam's father means by good and bad moonshine.
• how the book illustrations help the reader understand Sam and her behavior.

Ask your students what they would have done in Sam's place.

The House of Wings
Byars, Betsy
Penguin
1972

In *The House of Wings*, Sammy is left with his grandfather while his parents travel to Detroit to set up their new home. Sammy is extremely angry at being left behind with a grandfather he has never met. His anger results in disrespect to his grandfather and angry threats to run away.

Invite your students to think about and discuss:
• why Sammy behaved so rebelliously to a grandfather he had never met.
• whether his parents should have left without telling him they were going.
• the kind of person the grandfather was.
• how the grandfather treated Sammy.
• why the grandfather called Sammy "boy."

Ask your students how they would have behaved if they'd been left behind without being told in advance.

Tree by Leaf
Voigt, Cynthia
Atheneum
1988

Clotilde and Nate Speer's father has been facially disfigured during the first World War, and he now lives alone in a beach house on the Maine property that was willed to Clotilde. Nate tells many lies about his family and doesn't keep his promise to them as they try to adjust to the disability. Nate's grandfather supports Nate's separation from his mother and his sister.

Invite your students to think about and discuss:
- why the grandfather behaved the way he did.
- why Nate lied.
- how the grandfather and Nate might have behaved differently.

Ask your students how they might have reacted to the grandfather if they had been Nate.

Fly Away Home
Bunting, Eve
Illustrated by Ronald Himler
Clarion
1991

A homeless boy in *Fly Away Home* lives with his father in an airport. They have to be very careful that no one notices them and asks them to leave. They constantly move from one terminal to another to avoid detection.

Invite your students to think about and discuss:
- why the boy and his father are disobeying airport rules.
- why they have no home.
- how the pictures help the reader to understand homelessness.

Ask your students how they would feel about living in an airport.

The Sign of the Beaver
Speare, Elizabeth George
Dell
1983

Twelve-year-old Matt in *The Sign of the*

Beaver stays in Maine at the cabin he and his father built while his father returns to Massachusetts for the rest of the family. Indians save Matt when he is attacked by a swarm of bees. Matt is asked by the Indian Chief Saknis to teach his grandson, Attean, to read. It takes a great deal of patience on Matt's part, and a strong sense of duty on Attean's to achieve friendship.

Invite your students to think about and discuss:
- why Matt lied to Attean about Friday being Robinson Crusoe's slave.
- Matt's reaction to Ben's thievery.
- why Attean feels weeding is "squaw's work."

Ask your students what they would have done in Matt's place.

On My Honor
Bauer, Marion Dane
Clarion
1986

Joel and his best friend Tony do things together; swimming is one of the many activities they enjoy. The Vermillion River is close to the homes of both boys, but it's off limits to Joel and Tony because it's full of sink holes, currents, and whirlpools. Nevertheless, Joel and Tony swim in the river after promising Joel's father not to go near it.

Invite your students to think about and discuss:
- why Joel didn't admit to his father that he really didn't want to bicycle to Shared Rock.

- the kinds of things that can happen when promises aren't kept.
- how Joel argues with himself to delay reporting Tony's death.
- why the father accepts some share of the blame in Tony's death.

Ask your students how they would behave in Joel's place.

The Cay
Taylor, Theodore
Doubleday
1969

In *The Cay*, Philip is shipwrecked on a small Caribbean island with a native West Indian, Timothy. It is only because of Timothy that Philip survives.

Invite your students to think about and discuss:
- why Philip is harsh and angry with Timothy many times.
- how Timothy responds to Philip's unkindness and disrespect.
- what caused Philip to feel and think the way he did about West Indians.

Ask your students how Philip's attitude was changed.

Autumn Street
Lowry, Lois
Dell
1980

Elizabeth finds a close friend in Charles, the son of her grandmother's cook. A number of causes bring about Charles'

death as well as great sorrow and illness to Elizabeth.

Invite your students to think about and discuss:
- the behavior of the older boys toward Charles.
- how Charles reacted to the older boys.

Ask your students why they think Charles walked into the woods alone in the dark and whether they think the boys bear any responsibility for what happened to Charles.

The Shadow Club
Shusterman, Neal
Little, Brown and Company
1988

In *The Shadow Club*, Jared belongs to a club formed by those who always come in second. They are never first in sports, in contests, or in class work. Members of the Shadow Club feel frustrated and angry at their never-first status and group together to share their feelings. This sharing ends in ways the members never originally intended.

Invite your students to think about and discuss:
- the formation of the club. Why did members feel they needed to band together?
- how caring for each other created major problems. Why did this happen?
- what, if they were Jared or Cheryl and always in second place, they might do about it.

Next-Door Neighbors
Ellis, Sarah
Margaret McElderry Books
1989

Peggy has come to live in a new town and is going to a new school. To help make new friends, she pretends to own a horse in order to make herself more interesting. Peggy finds friendship where she didn't look for it and one of her friends suffers because of it.

Invite your students to think about and discuss:
- why Peggy felt she needed to pretend she owned a horse.
- why everyone needs friends and whether Peggy was right in what she did.
- why Sing, who disobeyed Mrs. Manning, his boss, was fired.
- should Mrs. Manning have fired Sing?

Ask your students what they would have done in Mrs. Manning's place.

Lyddie
Paterson, Katherine
Lodestar
1991

In the 1840s, 13-year-old Lyddie Worthen becomes a worker in a Massachusetts mill factory in order to make the money necessary to reunite her family and to keep their Vermont farm.

Invite your students to think about and discuss:
- why Lyddie and Charles disagreed, at first, about keeping the money from the sale of the calf. Why is this a problem?
- why Lyddie did not join with Diana in working to improve conditions in the mill.
- why, when Lyddie needed money so much, did she give her calf money bag to Ezekial.

Ask your students whether they have ever had to decide between pursuing something they wanted and, setting aside their personal goals, working with others for the good of everyone.

Bat 6
Wolff, Virginia Euwer
Scholastic Inc.
1998

It is 1949 and the 50th anniversary of Bat 6, a softball game played each year between the sixth-grade girls in two schools in Oregon. With the exception of two players, Aki and Shazam, one on each team, the sixth graders have known one another for all of their school years.

Invite your students to think about and discuss:
- Shazam's behavior which puzzled many people, but no one said or did anything about it. Why?
- whether they have ever been embarrassed by another person's behavior. What did they do about it?
- why Aki kept saying, "I'm all right. It's not so bad," when she obviously was not all right.

Ask your students what thoughts they, community members, family members, and teachers might have about how to heal the hurt and shock they all felt after Aki's serious injury.

Wringer
Spinelli, Jerry
Harper Collins
1997

Palmer LaRue does not want to become 10 years old because he would then be expected to become a wringer of wounded pigeons at the Family Fest in his home town. His bullying friends and loving father play roles in intensifying his anxiety.

Invite your students to think about and discuss:
- whether they have ever wanted to be part of a group so much that they acted in ways that made them uncomfortable, anxious, or guilty? Later, how did they feel about their behavior?
- how desperate Palmer's fear of becoming a wringer was. Despite that, he did not go for help to his parents who loved him. Why?
- according to those involved in the annual Pigeon Day shoot, wringers were necessary. What brought about this need for wringers? Does this make sense?

Ask your students what other ways a community might raise money to maintain and improve its local park.

References

Coles, Robert.
The Call of Stories: Stories and the Moral Imagination
Boston: Houghton Mifflin, 1989.

Coles, Robert.
The Moral Life of Children
New York: Harcourt Brace, 1991.

Bibliography

Garman, Charlotte G.
Taking a Good Look At Discipline
Elizabethtown, PA:
Continental Press, 1992.

Gilligan, Carol
*In A Different Voice:
Psychological Theory and Women's
Development*
Cambridge, MA:
Harvard University Press, 1993.

Kagan, Jerome
The Nature of the Child
New York: Basic Books, Inc. 1984.

Kohlberg, Lawrence
*Child Psychology and Child Education: A
Cognitive-Developmental View*
New York: Longman, Inc., 1987.

Lickona, Thomas
*Educating for Character: How Our
Schools Can Teach Respect and
Responsibility*
New York: Bantam Books, 1991.

Stern-LaRosa, Caryl and Ellen Hofheimer
Bettman
*Hate Hurts: How Children Learn and
Unlearn Prejudice*
New York: Scholastic Inc., 2000.

Vitz, Paul C.
*"The Use of Stories in Moral
Development: New Psychological Reasons
for an Old Education Method,"*
American Psychologist, January 1989.

Wynne, Edward A. & Kevin Ryan
*Reclaiming Our Schools: A Handbook
Teaching Character, Academics, and
Discipline*
Columbus, OH: Merrill Publishing Co.,
1993.

Harvard Educational Review
(Reprint No. 13)
*"Stage Theories of Cognitive and Moral
Development: Criticism and Application."*
Cambridge, MA:
Harvard University Press, 1978.